Keynesian Economics

Keynesian Economics:

The Permanent Revolution

Being an essay on the nature of the Keynesian Revolution
and the controversies and reactions arising therefrom

G. K. Shaw

PROFESSOR OF ECONOMICS
UNIVERSITY OF BUCKINGHAM

EDWARD ELGAR

Published by
Edward Elgar Publishing Company Limited
Gower House
Croft Road
Aldershot
Hants GU11 3HR
England

Gower Publishing Company
Old Post Road
Brookfield
Vermont 05036
USA

British Library Cataloguing in Publication Data

Shaw, G.K. (Graham Keith), 1938–
    Keynesian economics: the permanent
    revolution.
    1. Economics. Theories of Keynes, John
    Maynard, 1883–1946
    I. Title
    330.15′6

ISBN 1 85278 098 3
        1 85278 099 1(Pbk)

Printed and bound in Great Britain by
Biddles Ltd, Guildford and King's Lynn

For Jina – at last!

'The inevitable never happens.'
J. M. Keynes

Contents

Preface

The present volume is not intended to serve as a text although it does contain material of an essentially expository nature. Nor can it claim to be a genuine work of scholarship which has carefully assessed all the evidence and points of view before coming to a considered judgement. Rather, it is more of a reflective essay in the History of Economic Thought surveying those aspects of the evolution of macroeconomic theory and policy over the years which have held a particular interest for the present writer. Putting these various strands of thought together in one volume has enabled me to place my own ideas in a better perspective. To this extent its writing has been very much an act of indulgence. If it serves a similar purpose for the interested student then its writing will have been worthwhile.

I have drawn upon numerous sources and I hope that the majority are fully acknowledged. For any which may have escaped me or which have penetrated my own subconscious thoughts without receiving overt recognition I do apologise. I must also plead guilty to having plagiarised several bits and pieces from my previous writings. I hope what emerges may constitute a new dish despite the similarity of the ingredients. As always, I must place on record my special thanks to Mrs Linda Waterman, not only for the excellence of her typing and general secretarial services but also for numerous improvements in style and exposition. Finally, to Mark Blaug, I am indebted for suggesting the present title.

November 1987

1 Introduction

In the History of Economic Thought, two diametrically opposed viewpoints can be discerned, one undeniably optimistic and inclined to adopt a Dr Panglossian view of the world, that all is necessarily for the best, whilst the other is pessimistic and subscribes to a fundamentally Hobbesian perspective that life is nasty, brutish and short. The former can perhaps be identified most readily with Adam Smith and his belief in the all-omnipotent 'invisible hand' which, regardless of man's desire for selfish advancement, none the less serves to promote the common good. The efficiency of the market economy and its ability to secure an optimum allocation of resources resides in the belief that it generates the required information set which is sufficient to allow diverse economic agents to coordinate their activities to their mutual benefit and satisfaction. The corollary of this belief is the adoption of a *laissez-faire* philosophy and a non-interventionist stance for government – apart from the need to promote a climate of competition to allow the market to operate at its maximum efficiency.

At the other extreme is the view most readily identified with Karl Marx which perceives the economy – and in particular the capitalist economy – as fundamentally and inherently flawed and thus incapable of avoiding repeated descents into the abyss of prolonged and massive cyclical unemployment which ultimately will lead to the overthrow and denial of the system itself. From this perspective derives the socialist view of the need for strict controls and for the central planning of the total economy – or at least sufficient control over the commanding heights to permit the progress

1

of the economy to be dictated in comparatively elaborate detail. This is a view which has commended itself to many governments of the Third World economies despite the fact that the informational demands it makes are truly daunting for such economies. In the more advanced economies of the communist bloc this perspective has also encountered difficulties in providing an adequate set of personal incentives for economic agents who prove to be no less self-seeking than their western counterparts.

Now both these viewpoints have one feature in common, namely that each recognises that unemployment and hence the business cycle exist as historical facts. Where they differ, however, is in the remedy they propose. The classical view initiated by Adam Smith, and continued in the tradition of Ricardo, Mill and J. B. Say, sees such lapses from full employment as temporary departures due to unusual conditions – the end of war, the too sudden introduction of machinery or attempts at restrictive practices on the part of organised labour. In any case, the remedy is very simple: if competition is allowed, equilibrium will be quickly restored through the normal functioning of the market economy. All that the government need do is to provide the appropriate competitive framework. Today, this essentially utopian view has its counterpart in the New Classical Macroeconomics which again sees deviations from the full employment norm as stemming from lack of adequate information or misperception of the information itself. Again, the market economy will provide the requisite palliative; all that the government need do is avoid any action which might generate uncertainty and give rise to misperceptions of the true underlying trend of the economy.

In contrast the second view, which we shall identify somewhat loosely as the Marxist view, sees the business cycle as an inherently *deterministic* feature of the system which cannot therefore be rectified without eliminating the system itself. The business cycle is a logical consequence of the dependence of workers upon an exploitative capitalism which, ever driven by the search for profit, must inexorably precipitate the collapse into crisis. Translated to the world scene, a similar thesis of dependence is invoked to account for the increasing divide between rich and poor countries and once again the only solution resides not in the operation of market forces (comparative advantages) but rather in the overthrow of the dependent relationship.

Many economists are prone to view Keynes' great intellectual achievement as an ability to encompass these opposing viewpoints. For Keynes was perfectly willing to concede the efficient allocation function performed by the market economy – once full employment prevailed. He did not wish to see, nor did he advocate, a complex system of microeconomic controls. He was pefectly prepared for the market economy, left to its own devices, to solve the problem of resource allocation. At the same time, however, Keynes contended that the market economy was fundamentally flawed from a macroeconomic perspective, in that it could not guarantee that full employment and the full utilisation of resources could be maintained. Moreover, and more importantly, he could not see how the market economy would be able to bring about a restoration to equilibrium once a substantial departure from full employment had occurred. Keynesian economic policies thus reflected a combination of both interventionist and *laissez-faire* philosophy – which is probably the reason why Keynes has earned disapprobation from both sides. On the one hand, Keynes advocated increased government intervention, including the socialisation of investment, as a necessary step to bring about a full employment economy and to ensure that departures from full employment would be quickly restored by the appropriate demand management strategies. At the same time, he advocated that once full employment had been achieved the market economy should be left to itself to determine the allocation of resources in line with individual choice and freedom. The question of a possible conflict between stabilisation and allocation goals was not an issue that ever figured prominently in Keynesian circles; it was simply assumed that such a dichotomy could prevail without undue interaction of one element upon the other.

What has become known as Keynesian economics has been the object of considerable hostility from both camps. On the one hand, conservatives have taken issue with Keynes' interventionist stance and his advocacy of the 'socialisation of investment' and with some of the implications of his philosophy for taxation and fiscal policy – particularly the implications of greater egalitarianism and the 'euthanasia of the *rentier* class'. On the other, Marxists have been scathing about Keynes' economics and his policy prescriptions which they see as a last-ditch attempt to preserve a decadent capitalism from imminent collapse. In the present essay our concern is with the former as opposed to the latter. In particular, what we attempt to do is indicate the essential nature of Keynes' attack on the classical economic system and why he sought to deny the self-equilibrating system implicit in the classical framework. Precisely what the fundamental reason for Keynes' dissatisfaction with the classical economics was remains an enigma which has taxed his interpreters – supporters and critics alike – for more than half a century. Today, considerable controversy still remains concerning Keynes' fundamental theoretical achievement. What emerged and became readily identified as Keynesian economic policy, however, is far less problematic. It can be described as a belief in the ability of interventionist demand management policies, primarily fiscal, to govern expenditure flows in the economy so as to maintain high levels of employment and output. It is to this philosophy that Keynesians of all persuasions readily subscribe, and in this sense we can identify a broad consensus of policy activities which we may denote as being in the spirit of Keynes.

In the present essay we shall attempt to indicate the reaction which this ascendant Keynesianism provoked, first in the guise of the revival of the traditional Quantity Theory of Money, which was to lead to the important doctrine of monetarism as exemplified in particular by Professor Milton Friedman and other exponents of the importance of the budget constraint. Secondly, we shall consider the reaction of the more radical and more extreme form of monetarism implicit in the New Classical Macroeconomics which encapsulates a fundamental return to the virtues of the classical invisible hand – albeit in a far more sophisticated guise. In so doing, we shall have need to consider the conceptual advances made in the theory of expectations formation culminating, in particular, in the doctrine of rational expectations, and their implications for policy. Throughout, our underlying theme is with the Keynesian response to these theoretical counter-revolutions and how Keynesian theory not only resisted the challenge but also underwent a fundamental metamorphosis, emerging ever more convincing and ever more resilient. Today, the relatively sophisticated prevailing Keynesianism (arguably more in keeping with Keynes' original intention) is altogether a different animal from that naively propounded by early Keynesian disciples and its enhanced standing is largely a consequence of the monetarist critique. Nor has this process yet reached its steady state. The Keynesian revolution continues and all the indications are that it will continue to serve as a relevant paradigm which will influence alternative theoretical and policy-oriented proposals.

A subsidiary theme of this essay concerns itself with the way in which the reaction against Keynesianism has influenced the policies of the Reagan and Thatcher administrations. There can be little doubt that the Thatcher administration, especially in its critical 1979–82 period, was much influenced by the anti-Keynesian opinions and attitudes of conservative academic advisors and economists with decidedly marked monetarist leanings. Although it is not always clear that members of the government fully understood some of the more arcane arguments and implications, there can be no doubt that Keynesian demand management policies were jettisoned (along with the advocates of such policies dubbed 'the Wets') and in their place there emerged a combination of the medium-term financial strategy and supply-side economics.

A similar philosophy prevailed on the other side of the Atlantic where the Reagan administration pursued its own brand of economic thinking which quickly became dubbed 'Reaganomics'. The latter echoed the need for monetary restraint to control inflation together with calls for deregulation, less government and the provision of supply-side incentives. There was, however, a fundamental difference between the two economic policies, in practice if not in principle. In the United States fiscal policy was far less strict, reflecting possibly an understandable if misguided attachment to the concept of the Laffer curve with the result that the fiscal deficit soared to record levels. The feature was not lost on conventional Keynesians who pointed to the comparative success of the United States in being able to control inflation without generating the rise in unemployment associated with the Thatcher regime.

This concluding section of the present essay is not intended as an evaluation of conservative economic strategy, although doubtless some element of evaluation will inevitably seep through from even the most impartial observer (which the present writer cannot claim to be), but rather an attempt to assess how ideas culminating in the reaction against Keynes, no matter how imperfectly understood, did exercise an influence upon policy decisions.

2 The Nature of the Keynesian Revolution

INTRODUCTION

More than fifty years have now elapsed since the publication of John Maynard Keynes' *The General Theory of Employment, Interest and Money*, an event which more than any other signalled a remarkable transformation in economics. Within a decade, economists, and in particular those charged with the formulation and administration of economic policy, were imbued with an unreal sense of optimism. Belief that the business cycle was now a relic of the past, that employment could be maintained at tolerably high levels by judicious government intervention, gave the 'dismal science' the humanising influence which, for all its Benthamite Utilitarianism, it had previously lacked. The Keynesian revolution sanctioned discretion upon the part of the authorities and provided a theoretical *raison d'être* for the interventionist policies already being canvassed on essentially *ad hoc* grounds by economists in both the United States and the United Kingdom in the wake of the Great Depression. Above all, it transformed the status of fiscal policy and overnight gave the concept of the annually balanced budget a decidedly jaded and even antediluvian image.

That such a transformation occurred is not in doubt; that it was due to one difficult, imprecise and at times rather tortured volume by Keynes is again beyond dispute.[1] And yet, remarkably in view of all the ink which has been spilt in the interpretative debate concerning Keynes and the Classics, there remains considerable controversy as to what was the real nature of the Keynesian revolution. Indeed, it has been argued that the revolution was more in the nature of a Reformation given all the classical baggage which Keynes declined to throw overboard and at one extreme it has been contended that the revolution has still to take place.[2]

Far from there being a consensus as to the nature of the Keynesian revolution what has emerged over the years has been a series of conflicting and contrasting interpretations of the true message of the *General Theory*. Although it is reasonably clear as to what Keynes was trying to deny – the self-adjusting full employment classical equilibrium achieved by price flexibility in competitive markets – and whilst the policy corollary of the above is equally clear – government intervention to promote a full employment adjustment by a combination of appropriate monetary and fiscal measures – the nature of the precise *theoretical* grounds upon which Keynes sought to deny the classical thesis and lay the groundwork of interventionist philosophy remains subject to considerable dispute and controversy.

How is one to account for this state of affairs? How can one explain the phenomenon of diverse groups of economists, each claiming to be Keynesian and yet each disputing the others' interpretation of the words of the Messiah? In part, the answer is to be found in the fact that the *General Theory* is by no means an easy book to read. Although Keynes was indisputably a gifted writer, the evidence would indicate that

1 Many economists are prone to view the *General Theory* as essentially a continuation and elaboration of the economics of the *Treatise on Money* published six years earlier. This view is echoed, for example, by Leijonhufvud (1968) in his seminal work on Keynes. However, even if we accept this point of view, it remains the case that the *Treatise* was received with disappointment by economists at large and lacked the impact of the *General Theory*. It was the latter which gave birth to what has become known as Keynesian economics and without it, the Keynesian revolution would have remained stillborn.

2 Cf. Will Hutton (1986), whose provocative title for his assessment of Keynesian economics is *The Revolution that Never Was*.

he found it extremely difficult to write. Consider, for example, the following argument:

An increment (or decrease) of employment is liable, however, to raise (or lower) the schedule of liquidity-preference; there being three ways in which it will tend to increase the demand for money, inasmuch as the value of output will rise when employment increases even if the wage-unit and prices (in terms of the wage-unit) are unchanged, but, in addition, the wage-unit itself will tend to rise as employment improves, and the increase in output will be accompanied by a rise of prices (in terms of the wage unit) owing to increasing cost in the short period. (Keynes, 1936, pp. 248–9)

Moreover, it was written over a longish period of time (five years or so) during which Keynes' own views were still evolving. Inconsistencies arise which render it possible, by careful selection, to substantiate opposing viewpoints. Coddington (1976) summarises this well when he concludes that the meaning of Keynes turns upon

A view as to what is central and what is merely peripheral, what is essential and what is merely incidental, in his writings; in this way apparent inconsistencies and obscurities may readily be resolved, at least to the satisfaction of those adhering to that interpretation. (p. 1259)

The difficulties are arguably compounded by Keynes' deliberate avoidance of any formal mathematical model and by the adoption of concepts (such as wage-units, windfall losses, user costs, supplementary costs, etc.) and by definitions (such as income, net income, net saving, and so forth) which quickly disappeared from use in subsequent attempts at Keynesian expositions. Indeed, it has even been suggested that Keynes was not fully aware of what he was attempting to do or where the logic of his thoughts would lead him. 'There were moments when we had some trouble in getting Maynard to see what the point of his revolution really was, but when he came to sum it up after the book was published he got it into focus' (Joan Robinson, 1973, p. 3). The appropriate interpretation of Keynes would most likely have been resolved had Keynes lived to revise his *magnum opus*. This, however, was not to be and indeed Keynes participated very infrequently in the theoretical debates which followed the publication of the *General Theory*. Partly on account of illness (a heart attack suffered in 1937) and then his involvement as the leading economic advisor to the wartime administration, Keynes' involvement in purely theoretical issues was extremely limited.

Whatever the reasons, the fact remains that today it is possible to distinguish at least three distinct schools of thought who all claim to reflect the message of Keynes. The dominant school, which we may regard as portraying the conventional wisdom, is epitomised in the neoclassical synthesis which finds expression in the Hicksian IS/LM analysis. Here classical analysis is combined with Keynesian insights to provide an all-embracing theory. In this view, the classical model is shown to be essentially correct in terms of its underlying theoretical adjustment and the *General Theory* is revealed to be a special case – the case where owing to peculiar conditions, price and wage rigidities prevent the indicated classical adjustment.

THE IS/LM MODEL OF KEYNESIAN ECONOMICS

Within the IS/LM framework, an unemployment equilibrium cannot be maintained indefinitely given wage and price flexibility. If the existence of unemployment implies a decline in money wages, and hence also prices as unit-wage costs decline, then self-adjusting influences are automatically brought into being. On the one hand, the lower nominal value of GDP will require a lower volume of the money stock to transact it; the decline in the demand for money will imply a reduction in the market rate of interest, *ceteris paribus*, stimulating both investment and consumption spending as the present value of both capital and financial assets is accordingly increased. This influence was fully allowed for by Keynes and indeed has become embodied in the literature as 'the Keynes Effect'.

However, an appreciation of the importance of this effect is dependent partially on the interest elasticity of investment and consumption spending (summarised in the slope of the IS schedule) and may be relatively minor as Keynesian economists were inclined to argue. Moreover, regardless of the interest sensitivity of investment and consumption demands, it is clearly irrelevant in the case of the liquidity trap, where any further fall in the rate of interest is immediately ruled out. This situation constituted the Keynesian denial of the classical self-adjustment mechanism, even given the assumption of unlimited wage and price flexibility. But as Pigou was soon to point out, it was insufficient in that it failed to consider the change in the real value of cash holdings consequent upon the general deflation. This effect, later to be dubbed the Pigou Effect, and essentially the synthesis of the Real Balance Effect of Patinkin's monumental work (Patinkin, 1956) generates an increase in consumption spending promoting an outward shift of the IS schedule which is entirely independent of any interest rate change.

The Pigou Effect vindicates the classical belief in the ultimate adjustment to full employment equilibria and it provides the answer to the liquidity trap. In the context of the IS/LM model it demonstrates the impossibility of permanent unemployment equilibria – given the assumption of wage and price flexibility. Why, then, did Keynes ignore the Pigou Effect? Did he regard it as empirically insignificant?[3] This is a possible answer but not a convincing one when it comes to refuting a *theoretical* analysis; indeed, Pigou himself appeared to regard the Pigou Effect as a theoretical nicety but not a substitute for practical policy intervention. The Pigou Effect, of course, becomes an irrelevancy in the absence of wage and price flexibility. Indeed, one can identify in popular textbook expositions the frequent assertion that Keynes sought to deny the classical model on this very ground – that modern economies do not exhibit wage and price flexibility. Such expositions have at least one feature in common, namely, that their authors have never read Keynes.[4]

3 The Pigou Effect refers only to outside money – cash balances created by the government. Inside money holdings, created by bank credit, for example, are equally offset by an equal volume of inside debt so that the effect of price changes on net worth cancel out. It is because the government is a net debtor, having issued the money stock, that the Pigou Effect is positive.

4 Moreover, such writers appear blind to the fact that far from being Keynesian this is indeed the classical explanation for unemployment. Classical writers were aware of the observed facts of unemployment and they explained its persistence by pointing to a lack of competition and monopoly trade union power which inhibited the required degree of wage and price flexibility.

Keynes was not concerned simply to deny the classical assumption of wage and price flexibility as being unrealistic; he was attempting to deny the classical theory on its own terms, *including* the assumption of wage and price flexibility in his analysis of the Keynes Effect.[5] Nor, had this been the point he was intending to make, would it have taken five years of arduous activity; neither would it have accounted for his claim to 'believe myself to be writing a book on *economic theory* which will largely revolutionise ... the way the world thinks about economic problems'.[6] Perhaps the easiest explanation is that Keynes simply overlooked the Pigou Effect. This is by no means an impossibility for real balance effects do not figure prominently, if at all, in the Cambridge School's earlier expositions of the Quantity Theory of Money in which Keynes played a major role. Indeed, it is this lack of attention to real balances which constitutes the basis of Patinkin's charge that the Cambridge School never fully understood the machinations by which the Quantity Theory worked itself out. Simply overlooking the Pigou Effect would be consistent with Keynes' earlier work and the Cambridge School's way of looking at the world in general.

Pursuing this point of view leads inevitably to the conclusion that Keynes spent five long and tortured years trying to disprove the theoretical basis of classical economics only to fall at the last hurdle on account of a relatively simple oversight. It is not a viewpoint which one would expect to be endorsed by avowed Keynesians. Yet, paradoxically, this is precisely the viewpoint implicit in the Hicksian IS/LM framework which so many Keynesian disciples, particularly in the early years, were so eager to endorse. Keynesian economics became identified with the Hicksian simultaneous equation model, popularised by Hansen in the United States, and the Hicks–Hansen framework became the dominant vehicle of macroeconomic theorising for the next half-century. How is one to account for such apparent perversity?

5 Also Keynes gave attention to the beneficial effects of price reduction on export demand in the regime of fixed exchange rates which, for a relatively open economy such as the UK was not insignificant.

6 Letter to George Bernard Shaw, quoted by Moggridge (1973), Vol. XIII, p. 492, emphasis added.

First and foremost was the fact that the *General Theory* appealed not so much in terms of its theoretical consistency but rather for the policy implications which could be derived from the underlying statement. What so many devotees were anxious to endorse was the policy prescription, which whilst not novel in itself, had now been given the semblance of a theoretical rationale. Indeed, the *General Theory*, whilst a work of theory, bristled with policy implications. The assertion, for example, that the marginal propensity to consume would decline with increasing income (an assertion, it may be noticed, based on armchair reflection and unrelated to any empirical evidence) provided *a priori* the rationale for progressive taxation and income redistribution in favour of the poor as a means of raising the level of aggregate demand. At the same time, the concept of the multiplier suggested that even small changes in the level of aggregate demand would be magnified in their impact upon the macroeconomy. The appeal of the *General Theory* was precisely that it offered a demand-determined model and that the monetary and fiscal authorities possessed the means to control or at least influence the level of effective demand. In many respects this was the single most important point of departure from the classical economic system which, taking refuge in Say's Law of Markets had simply assumed that demand could safely take care of itself. The *General Theory* provided the practical thinking economist with a possible way out of the classical *laissez-faire* dilemma which maintained that nothing could be done to speed up the adjustment process already inherent in the system – nothing, that is, apart from allowing the forces of competition free play. In particular, the so-called Treasury View, which had maintained that public sector investment as a means of promoting employment was misguided because it had to be financed by withdrawing resources from the (more efficient?) private sector, was now seriously questioned for the first time. For what the Keynesian message seemed to imply was that, in a situation of deep recession, public sector outlays would so raise income as to generate the additional savings to finance the initial investment. There need be no net withdrawal of resources from the private sector *in toto*.

Secondly, part of the appeal of the IS/LM synthesis rested

upon the fact that it incorporated so much of the accepted classical economic framework. Despite new names for old – as, for example, the marginal efficiency of capital and the concept of liquidity preference in place of marginal productivity and the demand for money – Keynesian economics in its IS/LM garb was decidedly classical in spirit. The marginal productivity theory of distribution together with diminishing returns, the assumption of profit and utility maximisation (albeit with possible suggestions of money illusion) were all perfectly compatible with what had gone before. Thus the novelty of a monetary theory of interest together with the increased emphasis on the role of expectations appeared distinctly Keynesian but were not incompatible with the prevailing orthodoxy. The fact that so much of the classical tradition could be incorporated into the new Keynesian economics with an effective demand emphasis made it easier for the economics profession to absorb the new doctrine, especially where the underlying theoretical basis of that doctrine was not immediately clear.

Finally, whilst the Pigou Effect might provide the theoretical vindication for classical economics in principle, for all practical purposes it was an irrelevancy. Modern economies did not appear to exhibit the requisite degree of wage and price flexibility within a reasonably short time-horizon so as to deny the concept of a Keynesian unemployment equilibrium. As such it was no substitute for policy prescription along essentially Keynesian lines. Keynesians were thus happy to concede this theoretical battle whilst claiming to have won the all-important policy war.

THE GENERAL EQUILIBRIUM MODEL OF KEYNESIAN ECONOMICS

The conventional neoclassical synthesis which minimises Keynes' greatness as an economic theorist whilst simultaneously granting recognition to interventionist Keynesian policies (fiscal or monetary) was to be contrasted with the radical reappraisal of Keynes which emerged in the 1960s and is intimately linked with the names of Clower and Leijonhufvud (see, in particular Clower (1965), Leijonhufvud

(1968) and Clower and Leijonhuvfud (1975)). In this interpretation, Keynes is shown to have been pursuing a highly
aggregative general equilibrium approach in the grand
Walrasian manner but without the artificial and restrictive
assumptions which guarantee the Walrasian market-clearing
equilibrium.

The Walrasian framework views the economy in terms of
a series of mutually interdependent markets – one for each
and every good or service in the economy. A change in any
one market will generate feedback effects on other markets
because it will imply income effects for the participants within
the market undergoing change. This is the nature of Walrasian
interdependence; all prices are endogenous, being determined
as the outcome of a complex series of interdependent
simultaneous equations. What guarantee is there that a
solution to such a system of simultaneous equations will exist?
The Walrasian answer to this question is simplicity itself;
it lies in the adoption of assumptions which effectively rule
out any exchange or trading in any market at disequilibrium
prices. This restriction takes the form of the assumption of
an auctioneer who calls out prices for each and every good.
Participants in the various markets then respond to these
prices by indicating the quantities they wish to buy or sell.
In this way, a price vector is established for all markets within
the economy, together with the indicated supply and demand
conditions pertaining to those prices. However – and this
is the essence of the argument – unless the price vector is
such that all markets clear simultaneously, no exchange is
permitted to take place. Instead, the auctioneer revises his
prices according to a predetermined rule, namely to raise
prices where demand is shown to exceed supply and to lower
prices in cases where supply exceeds demand. In this manner,
the highly interdependent economy moves closer and closer
to the equilibrium price vector which equates supply and
demand simultaneously in all markets. In such a world no
false trading – exchange at disequilibrium prices – ever occurs.

This procedure generates a number of important
consequences. First, disequilibrium situations are dispensed
with in their entirety since they are never allowed to occur.
The focus is always on equilibrium. In turn, uncertainty is

eliminated; the future is always one of full employment and market clearing. Finally, no participant ever requires any information as to what market-clearing price should be in any given market. Knowledge of the market-clearing conditions is irrelevant to the ultimate outcomes. Suppose, however, that we were to pursue the Walrasian thesis of general equilibrium allowing for interdependence between all markets but dispense with the assumption of the benevolent auctioneer. This is precisely the scenario which Clower and Leijonhufvud suggest was at the heart of the Keynesian revolution. Thus Keynes is regarded as viewing the economy in terms of four all-inclusive and interdependent markets – the markets for goods, money, bonds and labour. Moreover, Keynes conceded, according to this view, that a price vector could exist to satisfy supply and demand conditions simultaneously in all markets – the special case of classical full employment equilibrium. But suppose this price vector does not obtain. Prices are established which are not market-clearing prices yet none the less a certain amount of trading at these prices will take place. Moreover, in the absence of the auctioneer, who in essence is simply a costless source of information, uncertainty will prevail with respect to what the market-clearing price should be. In the short run, at least, disequilibrium prices may be maintained with adjustment being thrown on the side of quantity changes. But such false trading will imply certain income effects for the participants in the market which in turn will generate feedback effects upon other markets. Some market traders will experience a reduction in income from what they would have earned had no false trading taken place, and in turn this will lead them to curtail their demands in alternative markets. In Clower's terminology, effective demands subject to such income constraints may fall short of notional demands – i.e. what would have been demanded had the potential buyer been able to sell all his own products or labour services at the equilibrium market-clearing price. The existence of false trading in one market, therefore, may so constrain income as to impose income constraints in alternative markets which in turn will generate further income constraints in the market exhibiting the initial disequilibrium. In this manner, the existence of false trading may lead to an adjustment path which is increasingly divergent from the indicated equilibrium. This, in Clower's view, accounts for the emphasis given to the concept of the multiplier as a destabilising device resulting from some autonomous disturbance.

The Clower–Leijonhufvud interpretation is ingenious to say the least. It is also strikingly at variance with the IS/LM model discussed previously. This is because the Clower–Leijonhufvud explanation of Keynesian unemployment rests upon the belief that comparative prices are in some sense out of line thus preventing simultaneous market clearing in all markets. What is required to eliminate the difficulty is a change in comparative prices. The IS/LM model, however, since it is constructed within the context of one homogeneous unit of output, conventionally labelled national income, is unable to deal with comparative price change *per se*. This is the reason for Leijonhufvud's repeated assertion (implied in the title of his seminal book) that Keynesian economics, as encapsulated in the Hicksian IS/LM framework, is completely at variance with the economics of Keynes.

Moreover, the Clower–Leijonhufvud interpretation provides yet another possible explanation for Keynes' *legitimate* dismissal of the Pigou Effect. The Pigou Effect rests upon the supposition that unemployment will provide a decline in money wages which in turn will generate a fairly predictable fall in all money prices. But if unemployment is the consequence of *relative* prices being out of line, general deflation, as implied by the Pigou effect, is of no avail. What is required is a change in relative prices and in particular a rise in the comparative value of capital assets to promote much-needed labour-absorbing investment. And this is precisely why Keynes pays attention to the so-called Keynes Effect of a fall in money wage rates. By promoting a reduction in the rate of interest, it increases the present value of capital assets (the demand price) relative to all other prices in the system. In turn, raising the present value of capital assets will stimulate investment, raising incomes (at fixed wage rates) in the labour market which will generate spillover effects in other markets, especially the goods market. Thus, Keynes is perfectly justified in considering the interest rate consequence of a cut in money wages because it promotes a favourable realignment in comparative prices in the direction of full employment. At the same time, however, he is equally justified in ignoring the Pigou effect in its entirety since by failing to consider comparative price changes, it fails even to begin to deal with the cause of unemployment. The Keynesian oversight is no oversight at all.

It is perhaps necessary to note that despite these favourable consequences of the Keynes Effect, Keynes remains opposed to any policy of cutting money wages. Again, the rationale is perfectly consistent. For if the beneficial consequence of money wage cuts reveals itself in a reduction in interest rates, the same effects can be achieved much more readily and much more easily by an accommodating increase in the money supply. A fall in prices with a given money stock is theoretically akin to a money supply increase with no change in prices in respect of the beneficial interest rate effects. However, whereas the former implies disruptive conflicts with the trade union movement, generating considerable social tensions over a protracted period of time, the latter can be achieved with immediate effect with no adverse repercussions. And by the same token, in those situations where an increase in the money stock has no real effect upon the rate of interest (the situation of the so-called liquidity trap) then a policy of cutting money wages will be equally ineffective. Keynes is explicit upon this point:

It follows that wage reductions, as a method of securing full employment, are also subject to the same limitations as the method of increasing the quantity of money....

There is therefore, no ground for the belief that a flexible wage policy is capable of maintaining a state of continuous full employment – any more than for the belief than [sic] an open-market monetary policy is capable, unaided, of achieving this result. (Keynes, 1936, pp. 266–7)

The Clower–Liejonhufvud thesis that Keynes was really attempting to deal with disequilibrium economic processes, without arguably being fully aware of where this was bound to lead, is an assertion that Keynes was making a revolutionary break with the established economic tradition and does indeed deserve the status of a truly great theoretical economist. In doing so, the emphasis is clearly upon the difficulties of the market economy being able to attain the indicated equilibrium price vector even though such a vector may, indeed, exist. Why should such a difficulty arise? The answer to this question pinpoints the true role of the omnipotent auctioneer within the Walrasian system. Essentially, as has been said above, the Walrasian auctioneer is simply a *costless* source of perfect information which allows the complete coordination of numerous economic agents participating in countless different markets for goods and services. The information set is so complete that all economic agents' decisions are always perfectly compatible with all others. Once the auctioneer is dispensed with, however, the information set becomes deficient, and moreover the acquisition of information is now a costly procedure. Agents will now participate in markets without knowing the equilibrium price. False trading will occur which in turn may generate false trading in alternative markets as income effects generate excesses or shortfalls in demand. In the absence of perfect information and given the existence of uncertainty, the sheer difficulty of coordinating the activities of all market traders in such a way that they are mutually compatible becomes a daunting and, indeed, impossible task. Of course, in this disequilibrium scenario, not all markets are equally important. The income effects arising from the existence of false trading in the market for hatpins can legitimately be dispensed with in the context of the macro-economy. However, in the case of more important markets – the labour market and the money market, in particular – there may be additional constraints which inhibit market-clearing conditions and perpetuate false trading. In the labour market, for example, considerations of equity or fairness or belief in appropriate differentials may prevent or delay the adjustment procedure whilst the money market may be characterised by speculative expectations which may in turn prevent the decline of the interest rate to its required level.

If Keynes' concern was really with the difficulties of gathering and processing the information required for the efficient functioning of the market economy, as the Clower–Leijonhufvud view would suggest, then it renders the *General Theory* incredibly up-to-date and light years ahead of its time.

Because today, one of the topics which dominates research agendas is simply the entire question of the information base of the modern economy. This has come to the fore in the wake of the rational expectations revolution which has taken place in macroeconomic theory together with the ascendancy of the New Classical Macroeconomics. Stated simply, the combination of rational expectations, competition and the New Classical Macroeconomics should imply the existence of continuous market-clearing in all markets. Faced with this conclusion, rational expectation theorists are compelled to explain the existence of the business cycle by reference to misspecification or informational errors upon the part of economic agents. In short, the New Classical Macroeconomics has been compelled to come to grips with precisely the same issue which obsessed Keynes – namely, the inability of the market economy to discover the appropriate price vector.

NEO-KEYNESIAN AND POST-KEYNESIAN INTERPRETATIONS OF KEYNES

Finally, in discussing the true nature of the Keynesian revolution mention should be made of a small yet influential school of economists who have emphasised the importance of expectations in Keynesian thought. In the United Kingdom, the Cambridge School of Economics, often referred to as the Neo-Keynesians and led by such stalwarts as Joan Robinson, Nicholas Kaldor and Luigi Pasinetti, has stressed the role of expectations and, in particular, the unstable nature of expectations influenced by capricious whim or unreliable information. Such fluctuations in business confidence impinge upon investment demand and render the market economy an extremely imperfect instrument for maintaining full employment income and suggest reasons for government intervention and control. In a world of uncertainty which follows as a natural consequence of unstable expectations time takes on a new importance. Time must be viewed historically and not just logically. It is non-reversible; decisions taken today cannot be reversed tomorrow; rather, one has to live with their consequences. What this implies, again in keeping with the Clower–Leijonhufvud emphasis, is that concentration on neoclassical static equilibrium situations is essentially misleading and irrelevant. It should perhaps be noted that the Cambridge School have extended the short-run Keynesian analysis to the questions of economic growth and income distribution and have thus extended their view of Keynesian economics well beyond the immediate concern of Keynes.

Similar, although far from identical, views have found expression in the United States, particularly in the interpretations stemming from Sidney Weintraub and Paul Davidson, co-founders of the influential *Journal of Post Keynesian Economics*. Again, the emphasis is very much on the importance of uncertainty and unstable expectations giving rise to the demand for liquidity and thus emphasising the role and importance of hoarding as a means of generating deficient demand conditions. Once more, there is a certain correspondence with the Clower–Leijonhufvud interpretation in that in the Walrasian system the existence of the auctioneer dispenses with the need for money as such. Any commodity may serve the role of numéraire, and what is therefore implied is a barter economy. To dispense with money and the role that money can play in a world characterised by uncertainty is, in this view, completely incompatible with the economics of Keynes.

THE SPIRIT OF KEYNES

We have seen that it is possible to take a number of distinct and competing viewpoints on the true nature of the Keynesian revolution. Upon what precise grounds Keynes chose to take issue with the classical tradition remains a matter of dispute. None the less, no matter how this question is to be answered, it is still possible to identify a series of policy measures and proposals which would generally be regarded as being in the spirit of Keynes. To this extent at least we can identify broadly what we shall term Keynesian economics. Its major characteristics would include the following:

1 A strong conviction that the classical macro-model

incorporating an inherent tendency toward automatic adjustment to full employment equilibrium was fundamentally flawed or required too long a time-horizon to substitute for direct interventionist measures.

2	A firm belief that the government, by judicious interventionist policies, could substantially hasten the process of regaining full employment in situations of recession or depression.

3	A belief that the macroeconomic characteristics of the economy were essentially demand-determined and that the macro-authorities should intervene so as to control the level of aggregate or effective demand.

4	A general preference for fiscal as opposed to monetary policy measures on the ground that changes in the level of government expenditures, taxes and transfer payments, provided a more direct control over the level of aggregate demand when compared to the rather uncertain and variable demand responses to interest rate changes.

5	A general tendency to discount the financial implications arising from budgetary deficits associated with demand management strategies, reflecting the belief that in periods of depression supply conditions were sufficiently elastic to enable changes in demand to be translated primarily into output changes as opposed to prices.

This then was broadly the consensus which emerged and became identified with the essence of Keynesian economics. In practical terms the policy emphasis was not as novel as has often been made out. As Davis (1971), Hutchinson (1978) and Bleaney (1985, 1987) amongst others have rightly emphasised, the utilisation of public works programmes as a way out of the depression of the 1930s was frequently advocated, particularly in the United States. There was little advocacy of wage cuts as a means of curing unemployment. None the less, the Keynesian emphasis on controlling demand gave a much broader interventionist rationale and foreshadowed the increasing encroachment of government control of resources. This, of course, was perfectly in keeping with the philosophy of the *General Theory* – the belief that the market economy was efficient in allocating resources at the microeconomic level but that it could not be left to its own devices at the macro-economic level. Keynes is specific upon this latter point:

I expect to see the State, which is in a position to calculate the marginal efficiency of capital goods on long views and on the basis of the general social advance, taking ever greater responsibility for directly organising investment. (Keynes, 1936, p. 164)

And

I conclude that the duty of ordering the current volume of investment cannot safely be left in private hands. (ibid., p. 320)

I conceive, therefore, that a somewhat comprehensive socialisation of investment will prove the only means of securing an approximation to full employment. (ibid., p. 378)

Together with the justification of progressive taxation and egalitarian transfer payments stemming from observations on the nature of the consumption function, the result was to provide a theoretical basis for an enhanced government sector and a far greater interventionist spirit to replace the largely passive *lassez-faire* philosophy of earlier years. It was not simply a question of a few random public works programmes to deal with the current unemployment problem which could then be shelved when they had achieved their intended results. Rather, it was a change in the entire outlook of what the government could achieve with an enlargement of its powers and responsibilities. Such was the nature of the Keynesian revolution.

THE QUESTION OF PRICE AND WAGE FLEXIBILITY

Regardless of the theoretical interpretation to be accorded to Keynes, the foregoing has emphasised the importance of wage and price flexibility and the ability of the market economy to generate the required adjustments consistent with full employment equilibrium. In particular, the classical model had assumed that wages would automatically tend to decline in a situation of unemployment and that in turn this would promote a downturn in prices until market clearing conditions pertain. In considering the Keynesian scepticism of this adjustment procedure, it is legitimate to ask whether there are any reasons to account for wage rigidity, on the one hand, and, even assuming flexible wage rates, whether there are any reasons for comparative price rigidity on the other.

Recent experience has provided considerable empirical evidence for the comparative downward rigidity of wages despite the existence of high unemployment. Indeed, recently, the United Kingdom has witnessed rising real wages on behalf of those remaining employed together with an absolute rise in the numbers of the unemployed. Clearly, the classical mechanism of adjustment to the market-clearing wage rate seems decidedly impaired. Are there any rational explanations to account for such a phenomenon? First and foremost, the labour market is fundamentally different from markets for other goods and services. This is a point which has been emphasised by Solow (1980), amongst others, and it stresses the role of convention and a consciousness of fairness and adherence to some form of social or moral code. Thus, for example, the unemployed worker seeks employment at the going market wage; he does not attempt to undercut the employed worker by offering himself for less. Equally, similar considerations pertain to the employer who is concerned with his public relations image and his sense of responsibility as an employer. He will not attempt to drive wages down during a period of extensive unemployment, nor will he attempt to replace existing workers by taking on the unemployed at lower wages rates.

Again, there are other reasons making for comparative wage rigidity quite apart from what is considered 'good behaviour'. Contractual obligations freely entered into by both parties may limit the room for manoeuvre. Trade unions, for example, exhibiting risk-aversion, may be willing to enter into long-term contracts at a given wage, suitably index-linked, as a form of insurance against a possible decline in real wages. In a similar vein, because of the high costs involved in hiring and training workers, and in particular the costs associated with the replacement of highly skilled workers, firms may be willing to offer substantial induce-ments, in the form of periodic incremental wage increases, to guarantee long periods of service from their employees. For many firms, it may also be the case that the wages bill is not a dominant element in total costs making for a degree of insensitivity to labour market conditions. For all these reasons the existence of unemployment will not of itself constitute a sufficient condition for a decline in wages. Indeed, it is possible that the labour market more correctly resembles the situation summarised in Figure 2.1 (where, despite the existence of unemployment measured by the distance Q_1-Q_2, there is no impetus to make wages fall) rather than by the conventionally sloped supply and demand schedules underpinning the classical model.

If there are reasons suggesting wage inflexibility, at least in a downward direction, there are equally strong reasons for believing in the existence of comparative downward price rigidities. Wage rigidity is in itself one reason to account for relatively stable prices. There are, however, a number of independent reasons for believing the prices, particularly of certain goods, will exhibit comparative price inflexibility and yet be consistent with rational maximising behaviour. First and foremost, the fact remains that changing prices is not a costless activity. Sales staff have to be notified,

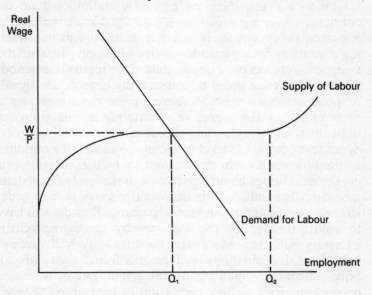

Figure 2.1 The coexistence of unemployment and static wage rates

customers informed, advertising programmes altered, and so forth. It simply will not pay the profit-maximising firm to alter prices every time there is some variation in demand, especially when the demand change has not been demonstrated to be permanent. Rather, the firm will respond by making a quantity adjustment, either by altering its production schedule or by changing the level of stock and inventory. In this way, elements of false trading may be extended over a considerable period of time. Again, even when the indicated demand change is of sizeable magnitude, the optimal price adjustment may be relatively minor and not worth the effort if the demand change is offset by a compensating change in costs conditions. Thus, over the course of the business cycle, demand and cost conditions are likely to move in the same direction, thus minimising the required adjustment for equilibrium. If, in consequence, the required adjustment is small it will not justify the costs involved in making the change and the firm will prefer to leave prices unaltered.

Quite apart from the costs associated with changing prices for business firms, there are equally costs imposed on the consumer. Keeping prices reasonably stable minimises the search costs for consumers and may be one means of attracting consumers to a particular source of supply. In a similar vein, certain prices must be maintained for reasonable periods of time if they are going to transmit the appropriate signals to potential customers. Moreover, price rigidity is also a consequence of the degree of uncertainty arising from the difficulties of coordinating decisions in a highly interdependent complex market economy. Consider, for example, a situation whereby in the attempt to reduce inflation, the government brings about a reduction in the level of aggregate monetary demand. A firm may well perceive that in order to leave output and employment unchanged, prices will have to adjust throughout the economy by the extent of the monetary deflation. Moreover, the firm may well perceive that its real profitability will be unaffected providing all prices, including input and factor prices, fall in the same proportion. Even if this perception is generalised to each and every firm and trade union in the economy, however, the question remains, which firm or which trade union will be willing to initiate a fall in its own final good price or union wage? In the absence of assurances that all others will behave in exactly the same manner, there will be a general reluctance to alter prices or wages; rather, once again, the initial response will be on the side of quantity adjustments with all the income effects that such adjustments imply.

The foregoing has suggested reasons for believing that comparative rigidity in both wages and prices is a normal feature of the modern macro-economy. This is not to assert that all markets exhibit such rigidities. There are certain highly efficient markets such as financial markets and commodity markets which more readily lend themselves to the fiction of the Walrasian auctioneer, by virtue of the nature of their product, and which presumably come very close to achieving almost continuous market-clearing properties. None the less, it does suggest that a dichotomy prevails between what Hicks originally termed fixprice and flexprice markets (Hicks, 1974). And it follows that a truly general macro-theory must be able to account for such a dichotomy and for the implied interaction that must take place between the two types of market regime. Economic theory is still far from presenting a convincing theoretical explanation along these lines, and if this is really what Keynes was groping towards, however uncertainly, the Keynesian revolution is still far from complete.

3 The Keynesian Ascendancy and the Seeds of Doubt

INTRODUCTION

Both in the United States and the United Kingdom, the Keynesian doctrine, at least as popularised in its IS/LM guise, quickly conquered academic circles. At the same time, the experience of full employment of the wartime economy, coupled with extensive interventionism and detailed strict controls, particularly in the UK, seemed to point to a Keynesian solution in indicating that government expenditures could secure a massive increase in both real output and employment. The wartime experience, which was accompanied by a substantial increase in the participation rate of the female labour force, undoubtedly played its part in conditioning attitudes towards employment policies for the post-war period. Both in the United States and the United Kingdom, even before the war had finally been brought to a conclusion, governments were committed to the maintenance of high or full employment in the post-war period. In the United Kingdom the White Paper on *Employment Policy* (Cmnd. 6527, 1944) made this commitment, whilst in the United States similar sentiments were ultimately endorsed by Congress in the Employment Act of 1946. Implicit in this commitment was the rejection of the annually balanced budget as an end in itself and a willingness to contemplate the possibility of budgetary deficits

28

as a necessary consequence of generating the requisite level of aggregate demand. In the United Kingdom, the experience of the wartime controls coupled with heavy taxation also contributed to a definite fiscal orientation being accorded to macroeconomic policy and a certain downgrading of the importance of monetary forces. Also, it was no doubt partly because of the ease with which fiscal measures could be enacted and implemented within the United Kingdom, that a decided preference emerged, especially within the Treasury, for fiscal, as opposed to monetary, control.

It was, however, the experience of full employment without inflation being achieved and maintained in the United Kingdom in the post-war period which appeared to provide the final vindication of Keynesian economics. Despite the difficulties created by the need for post-war reconstruction, together with the extensive and ambitious socialist programme to launch the welfare state, and compounded by an acute dollar shortage, the new economics appeared remarkably successful both in maintaining employment and boosting output. Although there were, inevitably, differences in emphasis, there was a broad general consensus between the major political parties of the desirability of demand management strategies. There was also a marked preference for fiscal as opposed to monetary policy, and indeed as time elapsed, the conviction grew that monetary policy was unreliable owing to the almost unlimited scope for velocity changes. This appeared to be the conclusion of the celebrated Radcliffe Report (1959), the most comprehensive and influential review of British banking and financial conditions, which announced the nadir of the traditional Quantity Theory of Money and signalled the ultimate victory of Keynesian economics. Similar sentiments found expression in Treasury circles where elementary macroeconomic econometric models, still in their infancy, chose to dispense entirely with the monetary sector. Likewise, an equally strong commitment to Keynesian economic policies developed within official circles within the United States, although here the conversion was perhaps less Pauline and it was not until the advent of the Kennedy administration in 1960 that the conviction became complete. The composition of the Council of

Economic Advisors and above all the highly significant
Economic Report to the President (1960) which explicitly
stated the case for Keynesian policies in the strongest possible
terms and paved the way for the subsequent record $12 billion
tax cut enacted in 1962 marked the zenith of American
Keynesianism.[1]

So complete was the Keynesian ascendancy that any questioning of the new economics now bordered upon heresy.
None the less, such questioning was to arise and it emerged
from two distinct sources. On the one hand, the view was
expressed that by virtue of significant changes arising in the
world economy there had been an autonomous raising of
demand. Thus, it was alleged, the maintenance of full
employment in the post-war period had been more a question
of good luck than good management. This view gained a
certain circulation in an important paper published by
Matthews (1968) which, amongst other arguments, pointed
to the impresive growth in world trade, well in excess of
the growth of output as a factor in maintaining full employment. Matthews' paper raised many issues and stimulated
a lively debate (see, for example, Stafford (1970) and
Matthews (1970)) but in and of itself it did not constitute
a major threat to the doctrine of Keynesianism. Whilst
arguably questioning the efficacy of demand management
policies, in fact, it confirmed the aptness of the Keynesian
prescription by emphasising changes rendering the Keynesian
policies unnecessary.

More insidious and more threatening for the status of the
new economics was the theoretical debate that was to arise
from the revival of monetarism and lead on, via the revolution
in expectations theory, to the neoclassical economics and the
justification for supply-side strategies. This will be the subject-
matter of later chapters. For the present, we shall consider
the claim that autonomous changes in demand conditions
allowed the maintenance of high employment in the
immediate post-war period quite independently of the
operation of macroeconomic policies.

1   Ironically, this massive tax cut was later to be endorsed by anti-
Keynesian economists as constituting the essence of supply-side
strategy!

Any attempt to list the most important factors responsible for the maintenance of a comparatively high level of demand in the post-war years would without being exhaustive, undoubtedly include the following:

The Displacement Thesis

The displacement thesis, associated in particular with the names of Peacock and Wiseman (1961, 1967), offers a socio-economic explanation for the rise in government expenditures as a percentage of national income following upon national emergency such as war or natural disaster. Stated simply, it suggests that in times of crisis, for example, the Second World War, resources are mobilised on an unprecedented scale, made possible by strict controls and intervention and a greater willingness in times of national emergency on the part of taxpayers to make the necessary sacrifices. Once the crisis is past, there will be some initial cutback in expenditures but not to their former level. This is because the apparatus for generating and spending revenues remains intact and also the natural resistance of the taxpayer has been blunted by the force of experience. Moreover, in times of acute crisis, as in the case of the Second World War, there is a greater cohesion and sense of cooperation between the diverse social classes making for a greater social awareness of the need for change and reform. The wartime experience also extends society's awareness of what it is possible to achieve by the mobilisation of resources on a massive scale. This thesis would accordingly suggest that governments' command over total resources rises not only gradually, as implied by the changing composition of demand over time in favour of publicly provided goods, but also in discrete leaps associated with extreme conditions. That something along these lines applied in the British experience following upon the Second World War appears well supported by the empirical evidence. It was also undoubtedly reinforced by the election of the Labour administration committed to an ambitious programme of nationalisation and social welfare, and also by the sweeping changes in direct taxation necessitated by the war effort. Now, to an extent undreamt of at the time of the writing of the *General Theory*, the system of income tax deduction at source extended to the majority of the working population.

Reconstruction, Marshall Aid and the Cold War

A second important influence in maintaining demand at a comparatively high level stemmed from the need for extensive reconstruction in war-devastated Europe, together with the Marshall Plan which provided the necessary means of finance, particularly in helping to meet the acute dollar shortage. There were doubtless political reasons for such generosity but the consequences were undeniable and helped to bring about a remarkable transformation in Western European countries not matched in the Eastern European countries which deferred from taking part. Added to these influences was the inescapable fact of the Cold War and the drift towards nuclear armament which committed countries to maintaining an increasingly high level of defence expenditure in order to provide the same degree of deterrence. It is not easy to determine the employment consequences of such expenditures, many of which are essentially of a highly capital-intensive nature, because of the indirect effects and spin-offs which are difficult to quantify.

None the less, such expenditures were accompanied by the need to maintain conscription which served to tighten the labour market in the immediate post-war period. The wartime economy had also witnessed periods of spectacular, if often improvised, technical change which arguably enlarged the scope for greater investment and innovation in the restructuring of the economy. The simple need to replenish stocks of essential goods and raw materials also gave an impetus to demand and to the promotion of international trade. Frequent rounds of GATT, and the formation of trade groupings such as the EEC and EFTA, all took place against a philosophy of liberalisation of world trade-flows, assisted, at least initially, by the maintenance of favourable terms of trade for the war-devastated economies.

LIQUIDITY ASPECTS

During the war years and immediately thereafter, rationing and wartime controls restricted domestic expenditures. Moreover, the war had been financed partly by the sales of bonds at genuinely low rates of interest – the latter reflecting patriotism upon the part of the purchasers. None the less, such financing gave rise to a degree of 'liquidity' in the economy. Victory Bonds in the United States and War Loans in the United Kingdom were assets which could easily be turned into cash to finance desired expenditures. The question of liquidity was one that was overlooked in the pessimistic predictions of most professional economists who were forecasting a return to the depressed conditions of the 1930s once the war was over. Nothing could have turned out to be further from the truth but then there was no comparable period in which government debt had attained so high a proportion of GNP, either in the UK or the USA.

THE IMPORTANCE OF AUTOMATIC FISCAL STABILISERS

One feature consequent upon the changes mentioned above was that the fiscal system now exhibited a greater degree of automatic fiscal stabilisation. The extension of the income tax paying population at progressive rates of tax combined with increased social security and unemployment benefits and other welfare measures, gave an enhanced fillip to the negative correlation observed between employment levels and fiscal deficits. It is easy to overestimate the impact of such changes, and indeed it has long been recognised that automatic fiscal stabilisers are not able completely to offset any autonomous disturbance (Musgrave and Miller, 1948). None the less, any element of automatic stabilisation reducing the size of demand fluctuation would be magnified in terms of its stabilising impact by virtue of the normal Keynesian multiplier. Moreover, the growth in world trade, to which we have already referred, may be considered to provide another element of automatic stabilisation. Whilst the increased degree of interdependence between trading nations renders them more susceptible to the destabilising impacts of autonomous disturbances arising elsewhere, by the same token it reduces the destabilising impacts of autonomous disturbances arising within their own borders.

The increased inter-country interdependence was itself partly a result of the awareness of the mistaken beggar-my-neighbour policies adopted in the wake of the depression. Following upon the Bretton Woods agreement there was a declared intention to avoid undue restrictions on international trade and to devise policies to assist balance of payments adjustment without recourse to undue measures of protectionism.

THE QUESTION OF CONFIDENCE

In a well-known passage from the final pages of the *General Theory*, which it would be tedious to quote yet again, Keynes refers to the importance of the ideas of economists and political philosophers and concludes that the power of vested interests is vastly overrated by comparison. Within a decade of penning these lines Keynes' own ideas were proving this fundamental truth. Not just in academia but also in government administration and the altogether more hard-headed and instinctively conservative business community, there was a growing acceptance of the view that because of the Keynesian revolution the evils of the Great Depression were now a thing of the past. Although concern was expressed at the possible inflationary consequences of the abandonment of the principle of the annually balanced budget, there was an increasing acceptance of the view that governments now possessed the power to prevent the slide into the depths of the depression which had characterised the 1930s. As time went by, and the post-war economy exhibited virtually full employment without any undue inflationary pressures this newfound sense of optimism appeared to be fully confirmed. Now of course, it is impossible to quantify precisely what this newfound confidence added to the buoyancy of demand but it is reasonable to conjecture that its effect was not insubstantial. Investment demands, in particular, could now take a long-term view without the need to discount the more distant returns almost entirely, because of the perceived dilution of the risk involved. Whether such confidence was justified is, of course, an entirely different question. The fact is that the confidence existed, and existed partially, at least, because of the publication of the *General Theory*. Keynes, in his grave, might have permitted himself a wry smile, given all the warnings he had uttered about the precarious nature of expectations formed on the basis of incomplete information or information not fully understood.

We have seen, then, that there was a number of influences making for a certain buoyancy of demand, quite independent of any attempt by governments to invoke the new economics. To what extent, therefore, was the growth and prosperity which followed on the culmination of the Second World War merely a fortuitous occurrence, or to what extent did conscious stabilisation policy play its part? In principle, these questions can be tackled by trying to assess the impact of budgetary measures and determine to what extent they were stabilising or otherwise. A number of studies were initiated along these lines which were interesting primarily in highlighting the difficulties inherent in the very nature of the exercise. It is also of interest to note that interest in the assessments of macroeconomic policy tended to coincide with the first faint signs that all was not for the best in the Keynesian world. It began to seem that the problem of coping with demand deficiency was not quite as simple as it might have appeared at first sight.

THE ASSESSMENT OF KEYNESIAN POLICY MEASURES

The attempt to assess the efficacy of Keynesian counter-cyclical policies (primarily fiscal) sprang from the recognition of the inadequacy of changes in the actual budget surplus or deficit as an indicator of the ease or stringency of fiscal policy. Thus, for example, since both government expenditures and fiscal receipts are normally endogenous upon income, the former being negatively related in the case of unemployment and social welfare benefits and the latter positively related (the positiveness being enhanced in the case of a progressive tax structure), the actual budget surplus/ deficit will fluctuate with the state of the economy quite independently of any discretionary action upon the part of the authorities. To illustrate, in the United States the Great Depression had been accompanied by increasingly large budget deficits which appeared to have little if any expansionary impact upon the economy. At first glance this appeared to lend credence to the Treasury view and to suggest that Keynesian policy measures would be ineffective in promoting recovery from the depression. In actual fact, as Cary Brown sought to demonstrate in a pioneering article (Cary Brown, 1956) it could be argued that fiscal policy over this period had been restrictive and essentially anti-Keynesian in spirit. Automatic shortfalls in budget revenues stemming from the depressed conditions served to mask discretionary changes in budgetary policy aimed at increasing fiscal revenues in a forlorn attempt to balance the budget. The remedy, in Cary Brown's view, was to measure or estimate the budget surplus or deficit at a constant level of income. Thus fiscal policy changes serving to increase the budget surplus at a constant income would be deemed unambiguously restrictive whilst changes reducing the surplus at a constant income level would be unambiguously expansionary. Having obtained an unambiguous measure of fiscal stance it should then be possible to determine the effectiveness of policy by simply regressing the fiscal change against movements in income.

Cary Brown's influential article inspired a host of contributions aimed at obtaining a precise measure of fiscal impact. In large measure, these were attempts to improve on his statement and they pointed to possible deficiencies in the constant income level approach. For example, to evaluate just the *change* in the budget surplus at a given income level without regard to the *cause* of the change could be misleading. Thus, changes in the level of government expenditure are normally more high-powered than equivalent changes in taxation; equally, it has long been argued that indirect tax changes exert a far greater impact than equivalent direct tax changes. Hence, it is theoretically possible for an increase in the budget surplus evaluated at a constant income level to be on balance expansionary in its impact if it were to be accompanied by a change in the expenditure/tax mix or the direct/indirect tax mix. In a similar vein, a fiscal change evaluated at a constant income level may exert a quite different impact on income levels other than the one invoked for the purpose of assessment. A change in unemployment benefit, for example, would presumably have a negligible impact on the budget surplus if evaluated at the full employment level of income yet its impact could be considerable when evaluated at income levels consistent with heavy unemployment. Critiques along these lines merely served to emphasise the difficulties inherent in policy evaluation; in particular, they stress the dangers of attempting to evaluate fiscal policy variables by reference to a single indicator just as monetary policy evaluation would be suspect if measured solely by movements in M3.

Partly to overcome some of the difficulties referred to above, many economists have attempted a direct appraisal of the stabilising properties of budgetary measures. Essentially, such measures depend on a comparison of the actual path of the economy with what would have occurred in the absence of policy intervention. If actual income fluctuations are judged to be less than what would have occurred in the absence of budgetary policy then the policy measures may be judged stabilising, and vice versa.

By far the most ambitious approach along these lines was the study carried out by Bent Hansen (1969) for the OECD which surveyed the fiscal experience of seven economies over the period 1955–65. His starting-point was to estimate the impact of the budget by weighting changes according to whether they are tax or expenditure changes, direct tax or indirect tax changes, and so forth, and then to subtract their impact from the observed GNP data. This provided an estimate of the 'pure cycle' – i.e. the hypothetical progress of the path of the economy in the absence of any budgetary changes. A comparison of the actual GNP data and the pure cycle GNP data with the trend growth of GNP (the average

GNP growth rate) provided a measure of the budget's stabilising influence. Providing that actual GNP data fall closer to the trend growth of GNP than the pure cycle data then the policy may be considerd stabilising, and vice versa.

Figure 3.1 illustrates the opposite situation, that of a destabilising budgetary policy which Hansen claimed reflected the experience of the UK (birthplace of Keynesianism!) uniquely amongst the seven countries surveyed. However, this conclusion raises as many questions as it answers. There is no great virtue, for example, in stabilising the economy around a given trend rate of growth if the trend rate is disappointingly low and consistent with unemployment. Secondly, Hansen's study suffers the defect of being unidimensional in its objective function. In the UK during this period, the macro-authorities were often using demand management policies to meet balance of payments objectives even though these were in conflict with growth and employment objectives. One can hardly be blamed for not scoring a goal if the goalposts have suddenly and arbitrarily been moved.

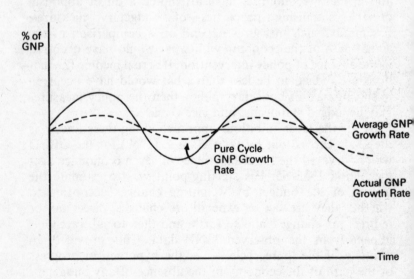

Figure 3.1 The case of destabilising budgetary policy

If one had to offer a general conclusion suggested by fiscal performance studies it would generally be along the following lines. Keynesian-oriented demand management policies have aided stabilisation and employment programmes in the post-war period if perhaps by less than originally hoped for. They have not been an unqualified success and have been accompanied by unfortunate side-effects, especially in the case of unexpected autonomous shocks such as those provoked by OPEC oil crises. None the less, there would be a fairly broad consensus to the view that in the wake of the Keynesian revolution, deliberately destabilising policies, which contributed to the event and duration of the Great Depression, have been largely avoided.

THE GROWING UNEASE WITH KEYNESIAN ECONOMICS

The empirical attempts to assess the effectiveness of Keynesian stabilisation policy reflected a certain unease that policies were not operating in quite so optimal a manner as envisaged in the theoretical model. Here a number of distinct issues coalesced to suggest possible pitfalls in the application of counter-cyclical policy. In particular, they suggested that the appropriate design and implementation of macroeconomic policy was altogether a much more complicated and demanding task than initially imagined. Amongst the major difficulties which soon became apparent were the following.

Structural Unemployment

In the United Kingdom, in particular, the post-war period was marked by an increasing awareness that certain staple industries had now lost their comparative advantage in the face of increasing competition on world markets, often from Third World economies, and were thus moving into a period of secular decline. Thus, for example, the textile industry in Lancashire, shipbuilding on Clydeside, and steel and coal mining in Wales and Scotland were all victims of adjustments in comparative costs conditions. Regional unemployment combined with considerable labour immobility was not responsive to general demand stimulus. The problem was no longer one of demand deficiency in a macroeconomic context but rather one of resource misallocation on a microeconomic level. In contrast to conventional Keynesian remedies, the indicated solution lay more in the sphere of regional policies. But such policies were often perceived – quite correctly in many cases – as but short-term palliatives to ease inevitable long-term painful adjustments. Moreover, they often suffered the drawback that regional expenditure programmes had unintended side-effects stemming from the location of the appropriate administrative offices. In any case, conventional Keynesian remedies did not appear to provide the answer.

Targets and Instruments

A second difficulty sprang from the recognition that objective functions were multi-valued. Straightforward Keynesian expositions had simplified the policy choice by conveniently thinking in terms of a uni-dimensional objective function, namely employment, which could be proxied by income or output. Given a target income level, say Y^*, macroeconomic policy then reduced to no more than adjusting the level of government expenditures and taxation consistent with the attainment of Y^*. In practice, of course, governments were confronted with the need to pursue other objectives simultaneously, such as price stability, economic growth and especially in the United Kingdom, balance of payments objectives. The first difficulty which presented itself was that of deciding the priority or ranking to be accorded to the various objectives when they were in conflict, as was often the case. Here the Keynesian theory provided no guidance, the question being one of normative as opposed to positive economics. Secondly, as Jan Tinbergen (1952) was to demonstrate formally, given a multi-dimensional objective function, it requires at least the same number of *independent* instruments as objectives if a solution is to be obtained which secures all objectives simultaneously. This complexity led to the search for additional policy instruments. In particular, Keynesian-oriented economists explored the question of prices and incomes controls as an additional policy instrument designed to improve the trade-off between inflation and employment by promoting a desirable inward shift of the Phillips curve. In so doing, they were to earn the derision of monetarists who looked on inflation as being a purely monetary phenomenon and who thus viewed price and wage controls as at best an irrelevancy and at worst a serious source of resource misallocation by interfering with the natural functions of the price mechanism.

The most serious difficulty arising from the multi-dimensioned objective function, however, was the conflict between the balance of payments objective and the employment objective. Attempts to promote expansion frequently ran into balance of payments crises as imports expanded ahead of exports. In turn, this led to reversal of the policy, usually by applying sharp rises in the rate of interest in order to defend the £. The so-called Stop-Go policy was inimical to investment and economic growth, creating as it did considerable uncertainty. Moreover, it ultimately led to the paradoxical situation whereby Keynesian demand management strategies were being invoked to protect the rate of exchange even at the expense of promoting increasing unemployment. This dilemma served to cripple the Wilson administration from 1964 to 1967 until the forced devaluation provided an extra degree of freedom. In Tinbergen terms, the exchange rate, instead of being looked upon as an objective, was in reality more in the nature of a potential instrument which could and should be invoked to secure the appropriate macroeconomic objectives.

Destabilising Time Lags

The IS/LM interpretation of Keynes was essentially an exercise in comparative statics with the time dimension of adjustment conveniently ignored. In practical policy-making, however, it soon became apparent that the lags in adjustment could constitute a separate hazard to the success of macro-economic intervention. The essence of the theoretical case that compensatory policy could be destabilising was initially made by Friedman in an analysis of 'lags in effect'. Taking account of the recognition lag – the time required to determine the actual path of the economy; the administrative lag – the time needed to devise the appropriate policy and obtain the necessary legislative sanction; and the lags in effect – the time needed for implementation of the policy measure and for the policy to generate the appropriate response – it is perfectly possible for the measure to start taking effect when the economy has already passed a turning-point in the cycle. Thus far from helping to stabilise the business cycle, discretionary stabilisation policy may actively enhance it. Friedman's conclusion, in keeping with his general political philosophy, was to eschew active interventionist policies and rely upon the gamut of automatic monetary and fiscal stabilisers. However, even this conclusion may be challenged for, with the adoption of suitable lags in the consumption function, it can be demonstrated that greater fiscal built-in flexibility can also be destabilising (Smyth, 1963). A number of formal mathematical studies, associated particularly with the name of A. W. Phillips (e.g. Phillips, 1957), invoked dynamic analysis emphasising the possibilities of perverse policy performance. However, whilst enhancing the complexities, they do not of themselves deny the case for positive interventionism. Rather, they suggest the possibility of the adoption of policies which may appear counter-intuitive providing the various lags are known with reasonable certainty. It is when the lags themselves reveal great variability that the possibilities of destabilising intervention become more acute.

The Problem Posed by Uncertainty

If the policy prescriptions deriving from the basic Keynesian model had any real failings it was because they viewed the world in altogether too simple a fashion. We have already referred to the fact that Keynesians tended to see the objective function as uni-dimensional with full employment being the only relevant consideration – at least in the early days of the Keynesian ascendancy. In addition, however, the elementary macroeconomic models on which policy prescription was based were decidedly *simpliste* in that they assumed that values could be given to exogenous variables and structural parameters and coefficients with almost complete confidence. In this connection, it is perhaps useful to distinguish between exogenous variables in the model which are under direct government control, such as government expenditures and rates of taxation, and those variables which might be regarded as truly exogenous, as, for example, variables determined outside the model, and independent of government control, as perhaps the volume of private sector investment.

Now, in the simple Keynesian models, the target level of income, let us say denoted by Y^*, is simply a function of the exogenous variables and the known coefficients, such as the marginal propensity to consume. If the values of the truly exogenous variables are known with certainty, and likewise if the parameters and coefficients are known with reasonable confidence from the study of time series data, then macroeconomic policy becomes a relatively simple matter of selecting the appropriate values of government spending and rates of taxation consistent with the attainment of the target income level Y^*. However, the real world is not as simple as this. In particular, the values of truly exogenous variables may be estimated with a considerable degree of uncertainty in which case uncertainty will also surround the values of the requisite policy variables. Optimisation strategies were swiftly developed to try to take account of these difficulties. Summed up in the concept of the *Principle of Certainty Equivalence*, they suggested ground-rules which sought to minimise the departure from targeted income levels over time on the grounds that this would minimise the welfare losses stemming from the failure to guarantee targeted income levels.[2] None the less, they created difficulties for the status

2 On certain restrictive assumptions, in particular that the welfare function is quadratic. Hence, a 2 per cent overshooting of the targeted income level is judged to have the same welfare loss as a 2 per cent undershooting.

of Keynesian policy measures. One difficulty lay in the fact that whilst a policy may be deemed optimal *ex ante*, it was usually the case that judging *ex post* an alternative policy had existed which was preferable. This aspect was compounded by the frequent adoption of minimax strategies which sacrificed the possibility of attaining the optimal outcome in return for the certainty of avoiding the least favourable (often unacceptable politically) outcome.

Moreover, the Principle of Certainty Equivalence, which was to figure prominently in the evolution of the doctrine of Rational Expectations (Muth, 1961) only dealt with uncertainty surrounding the truly exogenous variables. It did not, of itself, deal with difficulties arising from the mis-specification of parameter values. It may well be that major losses in welfare, occasioned by departures from the targeted income level, stem from the latter, giving rise to false estimates of the relevant national income multipliers. In this respect, there are two important issues to consider.

Essentially, the Keynesian approach lies in constructing a model of the economy which describes the manner in which the key variables interact to determine the general level of economic activity. The so-called structural model *explains* the way in which the economy behaves, in the sense that a theoretical explanation underlies the functional relation-ships. For forecasting purposes and policy simulation exercises we need to estimate the coefficients governing the functional relationships of the model. For example, if consumption depends on disposable income, we need to know the value of the marginal propensity to consume in order to evaluate the impact of a change in disposable income. Now in principle, such coefficients can be estimated by simply regressing past observations of consumption on disposable income. What is not so generally realised, however, is that even small discrepancies in the estimated coefficients derived from time series data can give rise to comparatively sizeable differences in policy impact. What is implied here is that the Keynesian concept of 'fine tuning' is perhaps 'less fine' than previously thought.

Secondly, and much more disturbingly, the validity of structural equation models of this kind depends crucially on the stability of the estimated coefficients. If the coefficients are themselves subject to change over time, then the value of policy simulation exercises using parameters culled from past data is immediately brought into question. But this is precisely what recent experience has suggested. In particular, during the rising inflationary period of the 1970s, when the applicability of Keynesian policies was coming increasingly under assault, it appeared that inflationary expectations promoted an upward shift in the value of the marginal propensity to consume. More importantly – and this phenomenon has now become established in the Rational Expectations literature as the Lucas Critique (Lucas, 1976) – it is argued that the crucial parameter values may themselves change in response to a change in the prevailing policy regime. If this contention is correct, it suggests not only that much Keynesian counter-cyclical policy is discredited, but it casts doubt on the validity of macroeconometric forecasting exercises in general.

Inflation and the Breakdown of the Phillips Curve

Of all the developments which called into question the relevance of Keynesian economics, nothing was so traumatic or as damaging as the apparent breakdown in the alleged Phillips curve relationship. This was partly, of course, because later Keynesians had so eagerly seized upon the Phillips curve to complete the Keynesian model. It implied a theory of price determination, or more accurately in the macro-context, a theory of inflation, which had been missing in the elementary IS/LM framework. It introduced the notion of trade-off whereby governments could combine inflation rates and unemployment rates so as to generate a constrained optimisation given some indication of the social welfare function. Moreover, it also suggested a new interventionist policy instrument in the guise of prices and incomes policies aimed at bringing about a favourable inward shift of the Phillips relation. The latter innovation was important in Keynesian thinking because it appeared to answer those doubting Thomases who had pointed to the possible inflationary consequences of unbalanced budgets.

The era of stagflation of the 1970s, which witnessed rising unemployment and increasing inflation suggesting a perpetual outward drift of the Phillips curve, was in many respects the last straw which for many people destroyed the confidence in Keynesian-oriented policies. The failure of the Phillips curve to behave in the required manner led to a fundamental questioning of its theoretical basis. In particular, Milton Friedman in a seminal paper (Friedman, 1968) contended that a function attempting to relate the volume of employment to the rate of change in money prices is essentially fallacious since it confuses real and nominal magnitudes. Since both the supply and demand for labour are a function of real wages, and are only temporarily influenced by the monetary variable in cases of short-run money illusion, whilst inflation is a purely monetary-determined phenomenon, it is clear that there need be no necessary connection between the two. The Friedman critique pointed to a natural level of employment, determined essentially by long-run forces operating in a competitive context, consistent with whatever rate of inflation was determined by the monetary variable. Whilst short-run deviations from the natural rate of employment could give rise to a negatively inclined Phillips relationship, the long-run Phillips curve would, to all intents and purposes, be vertical.

Friedman's paper was important in directing attention to the naivety of expectations formation implicit in Keynesian theorising – a charge that simultaneously had been prepared by Phelps (1968). As such, it may be considered as part and parcel of the upheaval that was taking place in expectations theorising in general to the detriment of the Keynesian position. At any event, the experience of the 1970s appeared to demonstrate the inability of Keynesian-oriented stabilisation policies to deal adequately with autonomous disturbances such as the OPEC oil price shock which precipitated a world-wide movement into recession. Defenders of the Keynesian position could and did respond that the recessionary movement would have been worse in the absence of Keynesian counter-measures, made possible by the willingness of the oil-rich nations to recycle their oil revenues. None the less, it was clear that consensus with regard to the applicability of Keynesian policies was no more, and a new paradigm was already waiting on the horizon.

4 The Emergence of Monetarism and the Economics of the Budget Constraint

INTRODUCTION

Keynesian thinking had downgraded the importance of monetary change. Implied in the IS/LM construct – given strict independence between the IS and LM equations – is the assertion that a change in the money stock does not affect spending decisions directly. It induces expenditures only indirectly by generating an interest rate change. Even then, however, at least from the Keynesian viewpoint, the response to an interest rate change may be weak and unpredictable, and further, occasions arise when the money stock change has no perceptible impact upon the prevailing rate of interest. What is implied in this analysis is that the velocity of circulation of money is extremely variable and the logical deduction which follows reveals itself in a marked preference for fiscal policy intervention.

Such a view was anathema to the traditional quantity theorist conditioned to perceive the world in terms of the equation of exchange with velocity rendered a virtual constant. In this scenario, any increase in the money stock would disturb the optimal holding of money balances and would thereby feed into expenditures, by one means or another, quite regardless and quite independently of any interest rate change. What is implied here – in strict contrast to the Hicksian simultaneous equation model – is that a change in the money stock promotes a shift of the IS schedule and not merely a movement in response to interest rate changes. The IS/LM schedules are interdependent.

In the early days of Keynesianism, this apparent conflict was resolved almost entirely in favour of the Keynesian viewpoint. Theoretical arguments were produced to justify *a priori* the interest elasticity of the demand for money, implying *ceteris paribus* the variability of velocity. Moreover, the assertion that the demand for money is highly interest-elastic is also an assertion that the supply and demand for money are interdependent and thus that the effect of an increase in the money stock would be offset by a compensating change in demand.

To develop this point more fully consider the situation depicted in Figure 4.1; we illustrate the classical view of the quantity theory of money, or more accurately the quantity theory of prices. The value of money, the inverse of the price

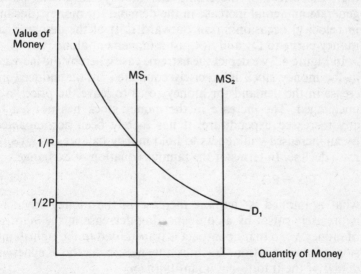

Figure 4.1 Traditional quantity theory – Value of money determined by supply and demand

index, is determined (as is the value of any other commodity) by the twin forces of supply and demand. Let us posit an initial situation where with a fixed money stock MS_1 and a given demand for money D_1 we determine the value of money $1/P$. Now if we increase the quantity of money, let us say by doubling it to MS_2, we generate a corresponding decline in the value of money $1/P_2$ as the price index rises to P_2. If the demand for money is drawn as a rectangular hyperbola, as classical writers in the Cambridge tradition were wont to do, suggesting that the demand for money was for a *real* command of resources in monetary form regardless of the price level, then we end up with the strict version of the quantity theory. A doubling of the money stock leads to a doubling of the general price level – a conclusion entirely independent of any consideration of the rate of interest.

Now, however, let us consider the Keynesian innovation of a monetary theory of interest rate determination. If an increase in the money stock ordinarily leads to a fall in the rate of interest, and if the demand for money is interest-elastic, then the effect of increasing the money stock will be to generate an actual increase in the demand for money (decline in velocity) occasioning an outward shift of the demand for money curve to D_2 and not just a movement along it.

In Figure 4.2 we depict the extreme case whereby the increase in the money stock is precisely countered by the induced increase in the demand for money so as to leave the price level unchanged. The increase in the money stock has not led to any increased expenditure; it has merely been accompanied by an increased willingness to hold money balances as interest rates decline. In terms of the famous equation of exchange:

$$MV = PO \qquad (4.1)$$

what is implied is that the increase in the money stock M is precisely offset by a compensating decrease in the velocity of money V, so that no impact is transmitted to the right-hand side of the equation. Such is the nature of the Keynesian denial of the traditional quantity theory.

The more sophisticated Keynesian approach to the quantity theory was widely acclaimed. Moreover, it was soon to be

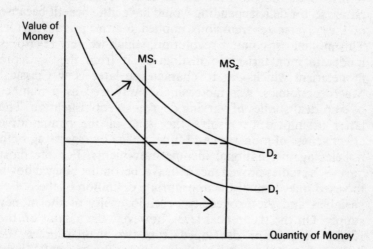

Figure 4.2 Monetary increase with interdependent supply and demand functions – the Keynesian objection to the traditional quantity theory

reinforced by additional post-Keynesian developments in monetary theory suggesting reasons why the demand for money should be interest-elastic in addition to the Keynesian reliance upon the speculative motive. Thus, for example, both Baumol and Tobin were to produce compelling reasons to suggest that the transactions demand for cash would be rationally interest-elastic (Baumol, 1952) and that normal risk-aversion would reinforce the inverse relationship between the demand for money and the rate of interest (Tobin, 1958).

The eclipse of the quantity theory approach to macro-economic issues was, however, to be short-lived. A resurgence of interest in monetary forces was soon to be awakened and to coalesce in what became known as monetarism – a belief that money matters and moreover is the dominant and overriding force in determining macroeconomic relations. Step by step with this development was a renewed questioning of the efficacy of fiscal policy and a growing belief that fiscal measures could be offset, or 'crowded out' in the current jargon, by inducing compensating movements in private sector spending.

The crowding out controversy was in many respects a return to the debate over the so-called Treasury view that public sector deficit spending would have little benefit because of the adverse repercussions implied for the private sector. This monetarist counter-revolution, which we may regard as moderate monetarism to distinguish it from the hardcore monetarism which was to characterise later New Classical Macroeconomics, was increasingly buttressed by a number of empirical studies of varying degrees of sophistication. The latter attempted to resolve the issue of the comparative effectiveness of monetary and fiscal policy by regressing both policies against national income movements. For the most part such studies proved inconclusive, becoming bogged down in vexed questions of the appropriate definition of the policy variables and the exogeneity or endogeneity of the money supply. On the theoretical level, however, the assault on the Keynesian position developed from two main sources: the restatement of the quantity theory under the aegis of Milton Friedman on the one hand, and a growing concern with the economics of the budget constraint and its implications for policy on the other. We shall examine each in turn.

MILTON FRIEDMAN AND THE RESTATEMENT OF THE QUANTITY THEORY

In 1956, when the Keynesian orthodoxy was virtually unchallenged in academic circles, there appeared, under Friedman's editorship, a most important volume entitled *Studies in the Quantity Theory of Money*, being the product of the Workshop in Money and Banking at the University of Chicago. From this time onwards, monetarism became almost synonymous with the 'Chicago School', an association which doubtless does grave injustice to the excellence of that academic institution. Perhaps in part it is to be explained by Friedman's claim that the University of Chicago was one of the few academic centres at which the quantity theory continued to be a central and vigorous part of the oral tradition throughout the 1930s and 1940s, where students continued to study monetary theory and write theses on monetary problems (Friedman, 1956) – a claim incidentally which was subseqently challenged by Patinkin (1969).

Friedman's restatement is all the more persuasive because of its stark admission that the traditional quantity theory, by claiming that velocity was a virtual constant, was incorrect. Indeed, Friedman takes great pains to demonstrate that velocity, far from being a constant, will respond in a predictable manner to changes in key economic variables. To this extent, at least, Friedman's restatement is very close in spirit to the Keynesian doctrine and at one extreme may be regarded as an attempt at a more sophisticated and complete restatement of Keynesian liquidity preference.

The other subtle change in Friedman's restatement also brings it closer to the Keynesian viewpoint. Whereas the traditional quantity theory of money had sought to show how an increase in the money stock would be translated into price changes in a fairly predictable manner, the new theory argues that the impact is now transmitted to a change in the value of money national income, with the change being either in output or price or some combination of the two. Again, this is not too distant from the Keynesian thesis whereby a money stock change may, by promoting a fall in interest rates, stimulate investment and indirectly raise output and employment. However, it is important to keep in mind important differences which produce policy implications radically different from those associated with Keynesian orthodoxy. On the one hand, the claims of the liquidity trap, whereby a money stock change has no interest rate effect, is explicitly denied. On the other, the division of the change in nominal GNP into its price and output components is essentially time-determined in Friedman's view. In the long run, monetary change is neutral with respect to the real economy and only nominal changes remain.

The most important feature of Friedman's restatement, however, turns upon the implications for the scope of velocity changes. In Friedman's view the quantity theory of money is essentially a theory of the demand for money, and the demand for money (which is, of course, a *real* demand as opposed to a nominal demand) is determined by a few key influences. Amongst the most important of these determinants are the level of income (permanent income in Friedman's case) and the rates of return on real and financial assets compared to the rate of return on holding money.[1] Thus, for example, raising the expected rate of inflation will raise the return on real assets and reduce the demand for money. In a similar way, raising the rate of interest on financial assets can be expected to reduce the demand for money. A reduction in demand is, of course, an increase in velocity. Far from velocity being a constant, as implied in the traditional statement, velocity will indeed respond to changes in key economic variables. However – and this is the crux of the restatement – such key economic variables are normally subject to only slow change over time. In contrast, the supply of money – the money stock – can be changed overnight depending on the whim of the monetary authorities. This leads to Friedman's classic restatement of the quantity theory to the effect that changes in the value of money are almost always supply determined. In Friedman's own words:

> It is clear from this discussion that changes in prices and nominal income can be produced either by changes in the real balances that people wish to hold or by changes in the nominal balances available for them to hold. Indeed, it is a tautology, summarised in the famous quantity equation.... The quantity theory is not, however, this tautology. It is, rather, the empirical generalisation that changes in desired real balances (in the demand) tend to proceed slowly and gradually or to be the result of events set in train by prior changes in supply, whereas, in contrast, substantial changes in the supply of nominal balances can and frequently do occur independently of any changes in demand. The conclusion is that substantial changes in prices or nominal income are almost invariably the result of changes in the nominal supply of money. (Friedman, 1968, p. 434)

The restatement concedes the Keynesian point that the demand for money is a function of the rate of interest. However, it is the *degree* of the responsiveness of the demand for money to a change in the rate of interest which divides the two camps. The Keynesian assertion that the demand for money is highly interest-elastic minimises the importance

1 Normally the rate of return of holding cash balances would be zero, although the rate could be positive in the case of cash held in a savings account or negative if held in a current account subject to bank service charges.

of the monetary variable for it implies that only a small decrease in the rate of interest would be required to induce a willingness to hold an enlarged money supply on the part of the general public. A small decrease in the rate of interest is unlikely to exercise a profound impact on the macro-economy. In contrast, if the demand for money is highly interest-inelastic, as revised quantity theorists would maintain, then it will take a substantial fall in the interest rate to induce a willingness to hold an enlarged money supply. A substantial fall in interest rates can be expected to produce significant repercussions on expenditures – both investment and consumption expenditures. Moreover, to the extent that political or institutional constraints prevent the required fall in interest rates to accommodate an enlarged money supply, people will find themselves holding money balances in excess of that which they deem optimal. In the attempt to adjust their portfolios, the excess money-holdings will be used to purchase goods and services or to acquire real or financial assets. Again, increased expenditures are implied, stimulating either real output ·effects or prices changes or indeed both. It is the increase in prices and output (incomes) which restores equilibrium; as income and prices rise the nominal demand for money rises accordingly until once more the general public's demand for money is equal to the supply.

THE POLICY IMPLICATIONS

It is, of course, in the policy implications of the revised doctrine that major interest and indeed controversy resides. In particular, the new form of monetarism raised again the issue of the comparative efficacy of fiscal versus monetary policy which the Keynesian orthodoxy has resolved firmly in favour of the former. The Friedman restatement posits that changes in the money stock are the primary cause of change in nominal income. The corollary of this position is that fiscal policy changes operating independently of money supply changes will have but a comparatively minor effect. Indeed, this contention is implicit in the concept of a stable demand for money function, implying stable velocity. For how is a fiscally-induced expansion of income, if not accompanied by accommodating monetary expansion, going to be transacted if velocity is relatively constant? This is essentially the monetarist objection to the balanced budget multiplier theorem. In the extreme form, with a fixed money stock and a constant velocity, any balanced budget multiplier-induced expansion of output requires falling prices. And yet falling prices are not a notable feature of Keynesian economics.

Friedman buttressed the claim of the primacy of monetary forces by reference to various aspects of the empirical evidence. In particular, he sought to regress *changes* in the money stock against the *level* of money national income and derived the conclusion that money supply changes peaked some 12–18 months ahead of the corresponding income level change, suggesting the strong *a priori* ground that the money supply is the causal factor in the relationship. However, Friedman's analysis has been criticised as being methodologically unsound and it has now been generally conceded that the fact of money supply change preceding income level change does not preclude the former being caused by the latter.[2] As long as the question of the exogeneity or endogeneity of the money supply is unresolved, the empirical data are likely to be capable of diverse interpretation.

Of course, it will be appreciated that the basic Keynesian model as summarised in the IS/LM framework is strictly neutral between the competing claims of monetary versus fiscal policy. It is only when one begins making specific assumptions about the respective slopes of the IS and LM functions that one derives either a monetarist or Keynesian perspective. Thus Keynesians emphasised situations where monetary policy is largely ineffective (liquidity trap conditions or interest-inelastic investment demand implying horizontal and vertical LM/IS functions, respectively) whilst monetarists are prone to point to conditions where fiscal policy is effectively crowded out (vertical LM schedules). The issue is an

2 Demand increases which stimulate the increased production of output, for example, will often generate demands for credit by producers to finance the production period. The response of the banking sector will give rise to increased monetary flows occurring ahead of the actual enlarged flow of output.

empirical one and again there are inordinate difficulties in resolving the weight of the available evidence.

On purely theoretical grounds, one might entertain a certain disposition in favour of the monetary instruments. There are two reasons why one might make such a claim. On the one hand, expansionary fiscal policy revealed in an outward shift of the IS function generates a raising of the rate of interest and thus, in the normal way, a certain automatic offset or crowding out of the fiscal stimuli. In contrast, expansionary monetary policy revealed in an outward shift of the LM function will be accompanied by falling interest rates which will reinforce the forces of expansion. Secondly, and here we encounter a subtle argument made by Friedman, a monetary change exerts a permanent effect in terms of the IS/LM model. In contrast, the expansionary impact of, say, increased government spending programmes comes to an end once those programmes are terminated. The outward movement of the IS schedule is reversed and it returns to its former position. In contrast, an increase in the money stock generates a permanent shift in the LM function; once the monetary stimulus has been injected into the economy there it remains until such time as the money stock ultimately wears out. And all the time, the enlarged monetary base is supporting a greater volume of credit money.

The modern restatement of the quantity theory also highlights the limitations of Keynesian theory with respect to the process of price determination. Indeed, in many respects this is the weak link in the Keynesian IS/LM exposition in that the statement is very much in real terms, and prices are virtually ignored or considered constant in less than full employment conditions. It is for this reason that the Phillips curve was eagerly seized upon by Keynesian economists in that it provided the missing link in relating inflation to the state of the labour market. Keynesian inflation theory is thus very much of the cost–push variety. It is due to institutional factors, trade union militancy or possibly rising import costs. In any event, it is not directly linked to prevailing monetary conditions. This viewpoint is diametrically opposed to the reformulation of the quantity theory. Indeed, the logic of the latter taken to its ultimate conclusion is that cost–push inflation is an impossibility. If the authorities maintain a given money stock, and if velocity is stable or virtually constant in normal conditions, a wage increase leading to higher prices in one sector of the economy must be accompanied by either unemployment or lower wages and prices in other sectors. Since trade unions are unlikely to behave in a manner calculated to leave their members unemployed, the general conclusion which emerges is that trade unions may be able to change comparative wages and prices but must remain guiltless of the charge of being responsible for inflation *per se*. In a similar vein, if the authorities are prepared to accept the consequences of maintaining a given money stock then some autonomous disturbance – for example, an OPEC oil price hike – cannot of itself fuel general inflation. All that it can do is to raise the price of oil-intensive products at the expense of non-oil-intensive output. Such is the logic of the monetarist position which renders inflation a purely monetary phenomenon. Of course in practice, downward stickiness in money wages and prices in non-oil-intensive sectors may make for initial adjustments on the side of output and unemployment. If the authorities are not willing to see the unemployment figures rise, they may be induced to expand the money supply to ward off the unemployment consequences. Thus, we may indeed observe the phenomenon of an oil price increase apparently triggering off an inflationary spiral, but in truth, from the monetarist viewpoint, the real cause is the unwillingness of the authorities to accept the unemployment consequences arising from less than perfect flexibility in the market economy.

We have seen that the reformulation of the quantity theory of money in terms of being a theory of the demand for money carries many implications for policy and equally challenges many of the conclusions of the Keynesian orthodoxy. As time progressed, some of the initial scepticism which greeted Friedman's reformulation began to wane and increasingly there developed a grudging acceptance of possible caveats to the Keynesian orthodoxy. At the same time, there developed an attack from a different if related quarter. Economists began to pay attention to the need to finance budgetary deficits associated with expansionary fiscal policies and began to be aware that the manner of this financing could affect the eventual outcome. Awareness of the economics of the budget constraint was to exert a profound impact on the analysis of the IS/LM framework. In particular, the fallacy of independence between the IS and LM equations could no longer be maintained. Recognition of the overriding importance of the budget constraint was to intensify the dispute between monetarist and Keynesian positions and, in particular, it was to lead to a much more sophisticated restatement of the Keynesian model.

THE ECONOMICS OF THE BUDGET CONSTRAINT

If Keynesian economics possessed one overriding weakness, it would surely lie in an over-optimistic attitude towards the consequence of policy-induced fiscal deficits. Indeed, the financial implications of Keynesian policies were largely ignored by Keynesian economists (if not by Keynes) who took the view that expansionary expenditure programmes would be reflected in output changes with prices largely constant. Even if such optimism were to be justified it would hardly excuse ignoring the manner in which such expenditures were to be financed. Much of the earlier Keynesian theorising, however, simply sidestepped this very issue, suggesting implicitly that the manner of finance was, to all intents and purposes, an irrelevancy. The rise of monetarism was accompanied by a growing awareness that the method of financing might be crucial to the eventual outcome. Monetarists frequently pointed to the naivety of Keynesian models in this respect and argued that by ignoring the question of financing – ignoring the concept of a government budget constraint – they focused only on the initial impact of a given change without paying due attention to the final outcome. The economics of the budget constraint was also of fundamental importance to the very essence of the IS/LM construct. Initially, in keeping with the Hicksian statement, the IS and LM equations were treated as being strictly independent of each other. Thus, fiscal policy changes would shift the IS function but leave the LM function unchanged whilst equally monetary policy would alter the position of the LM curve but exert no impact on the IS function. Given this assumed independence, the controversy in the so-called 'Keynes versus the classics' debate turned upon the *slopes* of the respective functions, with Keynesians tending to emphasise situations in which monetary policies would be largely ineffective whilst classical economists denied the efficacy of the fiscal instruments. Now, however, the nature of the controversy was dramatically transformed. The economics of the budget constraint exposed the myth of independent functions and reinforced the case for the crowding out of fiscal policy. Keynesian multiplier formulae were exposed as naive and incomplete. Moreover, consideration of the means of financing budgetary deficits raised the spectre of wealth effects which, again, carried implications for the effectiveness of Keynesian-oriented stabilisation policies. In addition, recognition of the force of the budget constraint carried implications for Tinbergen's Law; if monetary and fiscal policy were no longer truly independent then the policy-makers had one degree of freedom less in their formulation of macroeconomic policy.

On all counts the potency of Keynesian policies was being seriously called into question. Yet in retrospect, what emerged from this assault was a much more sophisticated Keynesianism, which although paying attention to the monetary variable, was much more in tune with real-world economics and much more able to deal with monetarist critiques. Perhaps it should also be mentioned that the economics of the budget constraint served to bridge the widening gulf between radical Keynesians on the one hand, and radical monetarists on the other. As Friedman has repeatedly emphasised, there is an affinity between his own position and that of Keynes, which has been increasingly lost sight of in the heated exchanges of the two camps. The concept of the budget constraint forced Keynesians to concede that money matters (a point which Keynes had never denied) without having to endorse the principle that money is *all* that matters.

THE NATURE OF THE CONSTRAINT

The essence of the government budget constraint can be summarised very simply. Total government outlays, whether in the form of expenditure upon goods and services or in the form of transfer payments have to be financed at all points in time by one means or another. The choice of financing reduces to either tax revenues, bond sales to the private sector or the creation of new money – which essentially constitutes bond sales to the Central Bank – or, of course, some combination of the above. More formally, we may write the budget constraint in the following way:

$$G + TP - T = \Delta M + \Delta B$$

where G represents government expenditures on goods and services, TP transfer payments, T tax revenues, ΔM the change in the high-powered money supply and ΔB the revenue obtained by the sale of bonds to the private sector. Since transfer payments can, conceptually at least, be considered as negative taxes, we may simply write the constraint as

$$G - T = \Delta M + \Delta B$$

where T is now to be understood as fiscal revenues net of transfer payments.

To bring out the implications of the analysis, consider Figure 4.3 which depicts a stable equilibrium with the budget precisely balanced. The upper portion of the figure displays the conventional IS/LM analysis whilst the lower portion depicts government expenditures as a constant and tax receipts (net of transfer payments) as endogenous upon income. As shown, we have a perfectly stable equilibrium at the income level Y_1 with no tendency for any change to occur. Suppose, however, that the government now embarks upon a programme of increased government expenditures to raise the level of income and employment along Keynesian lines. What are the consequences? In the upper portion of Figure 4.4 the IS curve shifts outwards and income rises to Y_2. This is the elementary Keynesian version of the story which monetarists consider seriously incomplete. The reservation stems from the fact that the

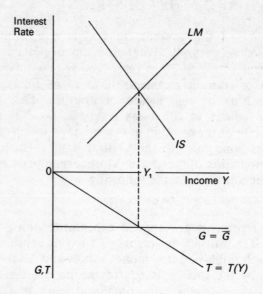

Figure 4.3 Stable equilibrium

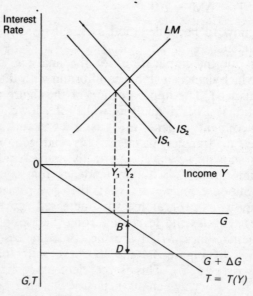

Figure 4.4 Deficit consequences of budgetary policy

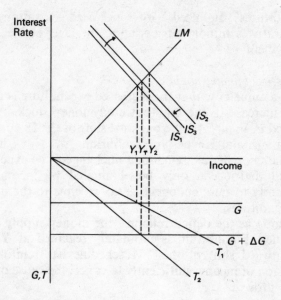

Figure 4.5 The tax-financed deficit

increased expenditures have produced a budget deficit, indicated by the distance BD in the lower portion of the composite figure.[3] How is the deficit to be financed? Let us examine each of the possibilities in turn.

By increased taxation.
If the deficit is financed by increased taxation this reveals itself as a downward pivoting of the tax schedule in the lower portion of Figure 4.5. Increased taxation shifts the IS function inwards as private sector disposable income declines. Equilibrium is ultimately regained at Y_T when the budget is again precisely balanced. The expansion of income from Y_1 to Y_T is still positive (reflecting the economics of the balanced budget multiplier theorem) but considerably less than indicated in the initial Keynesian solution. This is the essence of the monetarist charge that pure fiscal measures

3 The deficit is less than the actual increase in expenditures owing to some induced rise in endogenous tax revenues.

(expenditures financed by increased taxation) have comparatively minor impacts upon the level of income and employment.

By increased money supply.
Let us assume now that the increased expenditure is financed by an increase in the high-powered money stock. Again as depicted in Figure 4.6 the outward shift of the IS curve takes us to the initial Keynesian equilibrium Y_2. Now, however, with the tax schedule remaining unchanged, the expenditure-induced deficit can only be eliminated by income rising sufficiently to raise endogenous tax receipts to the new level of expenditures.

As long as the deficit remains, the money supply increase continues. Equilibrium is ultimately regained at Y_M when the outward shift of the LM schedule has reinforced the expansion of income sufficiently to cancel the cause of money supply growth.

Comparison of the positions Y_T and Y_M in Figures 4.5

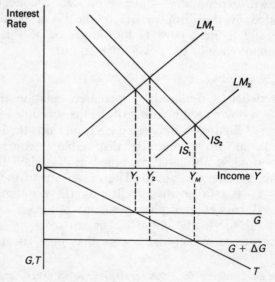

Figure 4.6 The money-financed deficit

and 4.6 respectively illustrates strikingly the monetarist contention that Keynesian-oriented fiscal policy measures which are not accompanied by accommodating money supply changes are comparatively ineffective. In contrast, when accompanied by the required monetary increase, they generate a much more substantial impact on output and employment. The implication is clear; fiscal policy *per se* is really an irrelevancy; what matters is the all-important change in the money stock. In this view, government expenditure changes are simply a means of bringing about the change in the money supply and might more accurately be looked upon as an intermediate step in the execution of monetary policy. In any case, the Keynesian tendency to focus on the income level Y_2 as being the new implied equilibrium is clearly in error and must be dismissed as naive.

This general onslaught upon Keynesian fiscal policy claimed many adherents and it was very much in keeping with the emphasis contained in the reformulation of the quantity theory. It also found some support in empirical studies attesting to the superiority of monetary policy – especially in studies emanating from the Federal Reserve Bank of St Louis which ushered in an era of rather dubious reduced form regression equations testifying to the potency of respective policy measures. It was also to lead, however, to a much more careful restatement of the Keynesian position and in particular to the reassertion of the importance of fiscal policy (Blinder and Solow, 1973). In this much more sophisticated approach it was to be argued (doubtless with the benefit of hindsight) that far from ignoring the financing of government expenditures, Keynesian economists had tacitly assumed all along that financing was by the process of bond sales to the private sector. And remarkably, this method of finance was even more effective than increasing the money supply as a means of stimulating output and employment.

To pursue this argument let us have recourse to Figure 4.7. Again, the initial increase in expenditures implies an outward movement of the IS curve taking income to Y_2 and creating the budgetary deficit. Now suppose the deficit is financed by the sale of interest-bearing bonds to the private

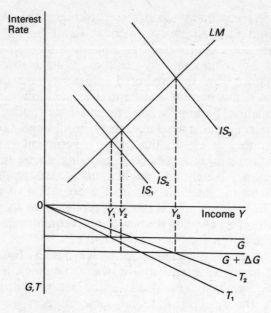

Figure 4.7 The bond-financed deficit

sector. Private sector disposable income is increased in
consequence inducing further rises in private sector spending
revealed as an additional outward shift of the IS curve.
Moreover, this additional outward shift of the IS curve must
continue as long as bonds are being issued to finance the
deficit. The process will only come to an end once income
has risen sufficiently to cancel the deficit. But – and here
is the rejoinder to the monetarist contention – the required
income level must exceed that associated with monetary
expansion. The reason is that the additional transfer payments
being made to the private sector in consequence of the
additional bond issue depletes the fiscal revenue yield.
Transfer payments being treated as negative taxes implies
an upward pivoting of the tax function in the lower portion
of the figure. Thus ultimate equilibrium is indicated at the
income level Y_B. This solution – the vindication of Keynesian
fiscal policy – does of course depend upon rather stringent
assumptions. It assumes for example that the government
can sell government debt without limit. Yet this may require

excessively high rates of interest which may not be feasible politically. It also begs the question of whether the continued issue of government debt generates wealth effects for the private sector which may interfere with the indicated adjustment. This is an issue which is decidedly relevant to the controversy over crowding out. None the less, it is a powerful result in the context of the Keynesian–monetarist controversy, for it implies that for any given level of government expenditure, the ultimate determinant of the income level is the rate of taxation as summarised in the slope of the endogenous tax function in the lower portion of Figure 4.7.

THE WEALTH EFFECT CONTROVERSY

The economics of the budget constraint was instrumental in bringing to the fore the issue of possible wealth effects generated by the issue of bond finance. In many respects this was not a new controversy; the essential issues had been raised by David Ricardo as far back as 1810 in his report on the Funding System, and then later repeated in his Principles of Political Economy in 1817 (Sraffa, 1951). The question posed by Ricardo was whether the substitution of bond finance in place of taxes (to fund the war against France) would have any real impact upon the economy. The answer which logic dictated (although practical common sense appeared to resist) was simply no. Taxes and bond finance would be formally equivalent in their effects assuming the private sector responded in a rational manner and perceived the future fiscal burden which would be required to service and redeem the debt. There are, of course, all sorts of qualifications which one must add to sustain this conclusion. Thus, for example, it is assumed that current taxpayers possessed of finite lives wish to make inter-generational transfers which guarantee their descendants a real post-tax wealth status. None the less, despite the caveats, the logic seems inescapable. How can society imagine that it is any richer simply because the government has issued some pieces of paper entitling the holder to interest which has to be financed from society's net resources?

On the surface, this conclusion seems damning to the very case for Keynesian deficit financing. Bailey (1962) has stated the crux of the argument in unequivocal terms;

> It is possible that households regard deficit financing as equivalent to taxation. The issue of a bond by the government to finance expenditures involves a liability for future interest payments and possible ultimate repayment of principal and thus implies future taxes.... If future tax liabilities implicit in deficit financing are accurately foreseen, the level at which total tax receipts are set is immaterial; the behaviour of the community will be exactly the same as if the budget were continuously balanced. (pp. 75–7)

Thus the assumption that government bonds are perceived as increasing net wealth by the private sector (however erroneously) is crucial in demonstrating the efficacy of Keynesian expansionary fiscal policy financed by debt. Why should such a perception occur? The simplest answer would be that the individuals making up the private sector are not as sensible nor as rational as Ricardian theory might suggest or alternatively are myopic in their judgements. Casual empiricism might well support such a conclusion. However, we can offer a somewhat firmer foundation to suggest that society in the aggregate may be led to such a mis-perception without exercising undue stupidity upon its part.

Any individual would be justified in regarding his personal wealth to include his stock of real assets, his stock of real money balances and his holding of redeemable government bonds. What is true for the individual will be generalised to society as a whole. Now when an individual gives up part of his real cash holdings in order to acquire additional government bonds his real wealth position remains unchanged and, indeed, he will perceive it as remaining unchanged. He has merely altered the composition of his portfolio. The same perception will be experienced by all people acquiring additional bonds in exchange for giving up cash. However, when the government spends the proceeds – which is the *raison d'être* for the exercise – society's collective holding of real money balances (providing prices remain unchanged) will be restored to its former level. Thus, all that has changed, from the perception of the private sector, is a net increase in its holding of redeemable government bonds and hence it experiences a positive net wealth effect. Keynesian fiscal policy thus relies on a dual premise, namely that debt financing gives rise to wealth effects as perceived by the private sector in its holding of government bonds and that the expansionary impetus is translated into output changes and not prices changes. In the event of the latter, the real value of the private sector's cash holdings would decline, offsetting the wealth effect.

The more rational economic agents are, and the more correctly they perceive the implications of government debt financing, the more they are aware of the true economic model underlying the economy, the less they will be misled by imagined wealth effects and the weaker will be the potency of Keynesian fiscal policy. It is hardly surprising that the expectations revolution in macroeconomics, culminating in the doctrine of Rational Expectations which imparts ultra-rationality to utility-maximising economic agents, is so fundamentally at variance with the Keynesian policy prescription.

Finally, to confuse the issue still further, it may be noted that a monetarist argument disputing the potency of Keynesian fiscal policy has been raised which depends upon the very existence of perceived wealth effects. Private sector wealth effects induce additional spending and thus promote a further outward shift of the IS function. In the context of Figure 4.7, this additional outward shift of the IS curve implies that the amount of bonds sales required for equilibrium is less than before. However, by the same token, the wealth effect may promote an increased demand for money, thus promoting an inward shift of the LM function and raising the amount of bonds sales required to attain equilibrium at Y_B. If the sensitivity of the demand for money to wealth exceeds that of consumption demands (and here Friedman's work on the high income elasticity of money demand is suggestive), then the inward shift of the LM function will more than compensate for the outward shift of the IS function and wealth effects will weaken the potency of fiscal policy. This argument takes on renewed force, if there is a limit, political or otherwise, to the volume of additional bonds that the government can realistically float.

THE DEBATE OVER CROWDING OUT

We are now in a position to review briefly one of the major issues surrounding expansionary fiscal policy, namely the charge that it may prove ineffective by inducing offsetting compensatory action by the private sector. The most obvious example of crowding out occurs when increased public sector spending by the government provides a good or service which competes directly with those provided by the market economy. In such a case, consumers may choose the public provision, often provided at zero cost as in the case of education and medical services, and cease to consume the privately marketed service. In this example, the increased public expenditure is negated in its impact by inducing an increase in private sector savings. In re-reading Keynes, it is immediately apparent that he was indeed aware of this possibility and it accounts for his advocacy of 'wasteful' public expenditures and his reference to the wisdom of Ancient Egypt which

> was doubly fortunate, and doubtless owed to this its fabled wealth, in that it possessed *two* activities, namely, pyramid-building as well as the search for the precious metals, the fruits of which, since they could not serve the needs of man by being consumed, did not stale with abundance. (Keynes, 1936, p. 131)

Secondly, there is the element of indirect crowding out, fully allowed for in Keynesian economics, which hinges upon the interest rate change arising in the wake of expansionary fiscal policy. An increase in government expenditures, or a decrease in taxation will promote an outward shift of the IS function. However, given a fixed money stock and a positively inclined LM schedule, there must follow a rise in the rate of interest which chokes off, in part, a certain proportion of private sector spending. *Ceteris paribus*, the degree of such crowding out will be less the greater the interest elasticity of the demand for money (minimising as it does the interest rate change), and the greater the insensitivity of private sector spending to interest rate change – both avowedly Keynesian assertions. In contrast, crowding out is greater the less interest-elastic is the demand for money, and indeed becomes complete in the case of a vertically-sloped LM curve.

Finally, we have *financial* crowding out which refers to the manner in which the government deficit is to be financed. Both Keynesians and monetarists would agree that crowding out is substantial in the case of tax financing whilst it is negative in the case of monetary-financed deficits. Where the dispute remains is in the case of bond-financed deficits. Ultra-rational behaviour, minimising the scope of wealth perceptions, reinforces the case for crowding out. Just how rational is the private sector, and exactly how sensible in its formation of expectations concerning the future progress of the economy, remains the subject-matter of the following chapter.

5 The Expectations Revolution in Macroeconomics

INTRODUCTION

If it were possible to summarise the evolution of Keynes' thinking on economics in one sentence, it would probably be in terms of the growing awareness of the importance of expectations in governing and shaping the progress of the economy. In the *Tract on Monetary Reform* (1923), expectations enter as an additional independent variable to reinforce the inflationary process set in motion by monetary expansion. Doubtless influenced by the German inflationary experience of 1919–23, the expectation of inflation leads to an increase in velocity as agents attempt to rid themselves of a rapidly depreciating asset. In the *Treatise on Money* (1930) the role of expectations emerges in a more dramatic form, for now it is able to generate an inflationary or deflationary process without the need for any monetary expansion or contraction. The divergence of investment from saving is shown to be an independent element in the determination of prices and such divergence may occur in consequence of interest rate movements arising from changing expectations concerning security prices in capital markets. It is in the *General Theory*, however, that expectations really come into their own, for now, they are solely responsible for the phenomenon of the business cycle by precipitating

72

a sudden collapse of the marginal efficiency of capital. As traumatic as Jevons' sunspot theory without its predictability is perhaps one way to encapsulate the Keynesian doctrine. Moreover, changing expectations concerning future prospective yields is the dominant force in determining the marginal efficiency of capital and far outweighs any compensating movements in the rate of interest. Indeed, for Keynes, the causal sequence is very clear; a collapse of confidence generates a downturn and by creating uncertainty over the future generates a *raising* of the rate of interest reinforcing the slump.

We have seen above that the marginal efficiency of capital depends... on current expectations as to the future yield of capital goods... the basis for such expectations is very precarious. Being based on shifting and unreliable evidence, they are subject to sudden and violent changes.

Now we have been accustomed in explaining the 'crisis' to lay stress on the rising tendency of the rate of interest.... I suggest that a more typical, and often the predominant explanation of the crisis is, not primarily a rise in the rate of interest, but a sudden collapse in the marginal efficiency of capital...

Moreover, the dismay and uncertainty as to the future which accompanied a collapse in the marginal efficiency of capital naturally precipitates a sharp increase in liquidity preference – and hence a rise in the rate of interest. (Keynes, 1936, pp. 315–16)

The downgrading of the role of the rate of interest in initiating the slump implies also a more limited scope for monetary policy in countering the slump. It points to the potential role of fiscal policy in maintaining confidence in future yields.

EXPECTATIONS IN THE *GENERAL THEORY*

The emphasis on the unstable nature of long-term expectations was undoubtedly a distinguishing feature of Keynesian economics. It was *the feature* which Keynes sought to stress in his famous defence of the *General Theory* to his critics in his *Quarterly Journal of Economics* article (Keynes, 1937).[1] There can be little doubt that by focusing

---

1 The critics were Leontief, Robertson, Taussig and Viner although it was against the latter's 'Mr. Keynes on the Causes of Unemployment' (Viner, 1936) that Keynes sought to direct most of his comments.

on the reasons why long-term expectations should be subject to such unstable behaviour in the short run, Keynes made a significant departure from the classical and neoclassical world of unimpeded adjustment to stable equilibrium. Furthermore, there are many revealing insights into the reasons why expectations are subject to such sweeping revision. In particular, Keynes points to the destabilising nature of the stock exchange where rational financial behaviour on the part of investors need have no real connection with the true valuation of the worth of real assets. This feature is compounded by the increasing divorce between ownership and control characteristic of modern industrial society. The actual owners of enterprise may have virtually no connection with the day-to-day running of the enterprise and no real knowledge of the true value of the assets they own. They may be heavily dependent on information dispersed by management which in turn may be self-seeking and lacking in objectivity. Again, the force of unforeseen competition is another factor which may lead to a sudden revision in the expected return of investment in a given asset. This analysis, which is remarkably similar in some respects to Chamberlin's thesis of Monopolistic Competition (Chamberlin, 1933) points to a situation whereby an investor may correctly perceive a worthwhile investment opportunity if he is allowed to pursue the activity in isolation but which turns out to be entirely unprofitable when the same investment decision is taken by others. All this is highly stimulating and suggestive, and constitutes a radical departure from the conventional neoclassical world with its emphasis on certainty. And yet despite all of this, there remains a certain unease concerning the treatment of expectations in the *General Theory*.

In the formation of expectations about future events we can distinguish between two different types of situation. On the one hand, we have situations distinguished by risk where recourse can be had to probability theory and, in particular, conditional probability. Thus, for example, in determining the expected value of a series of throwings of an unbiased die, elementary probability theory will suffice. If the die were biased in some known manner we would simply incorporate that knowledge in deriving the conditional probability of its expected value. This is the path pursued by rational expectations theorists and it leads to the holding of expectations which are efficient in the sense of minimising the variance of actual outcomes from expected outcomes. However, Keynes' concern is not primarily with situations comprising risk. Rather it is dominated by conditions of uncertainty where probability theory is no longer applicable. There is simply no scientific basis to formulate any expectation of the outcome.

It is with this latter consideration that Keynes is primarily concerned. In his view, the valuation of the present value of an asset, especially an asset with a relatively long life, is determined by influences which are subject to considerable uncertainty. Given uncertainty, expected values of given outcomes are not really quantifiable in any objective mathematical sense. Keynes is emphatic upon this issue.

By 'uncertain' knowledge, let me explain, I do not mean merely to distinguish what is known for certain from what is only probable. The game of roulette is not subject, in this sense, to uncertainty; nor is the prospect of a Victory bond being drawn. Or, again, the expectation of life is only slightly uncertain. Even the weather is only moderately uncertain. The sense in which I am using the term is that in which the prospect of a European war is uncertain, or the price of copper and the rate of interest twenty years hence, or the obsolescence of a new invention, or the position of private wealth owners in the social system in 1970. About these matters there is no scientific basis on which to form any calculable probability whatever. We simply do not know. (Keynes, 1937, pp. 213–14)

In such a world, expectations reduce to no more than guesses based on minimal information sets. Moreover they are held with little confidence and are thus subject to rapid revision in the light of any change in the prevailing economic climate. They are expectations lacking in any objective empirical foundation and as such are basically unstable and subject to capricious changes in sentiment or whim.

If uncertainty could be dispensed with, it would render expectations formation an objective and rational process related to empirically known facts. Equally, it would annihilate many of the reasons for holding money balances in excess of one's immediate transactions needs and thus eliminate a cause of demand deficiency. But this is not the world of Keynes. Liquidity preference is itself a reflection of the fact of uncertainty.

Having laid so much store by the importance of expectations it then comes as an anticlimax to realise that Keynes possesses no objective means by which to model their formation. Indeed, this is a natural consequence of his approach; how is one to model 'animal spirits' or whim or chance? Nothing remains but to impose expectations on his theory as exogenous elements capable of sudden, often dramatic change, but not in consequence of the workings of the model analysis. Hicks has made this point explicitly:

> expectations do appear in the *General Theory* but (in the main) they appear as *data*, as autonomous influences that come in from outside, not as elements that are moulded in the course of the process that is being analysed. (Hicks, 1969, p. 313)

If we are discussing the prospect of a European war or the rate of interest twenty years hence, this indeed might be the appropriate view to hold. But is it necessary for all issues impinging upon expectations concerning the future path of the economy? Yet this is very much the Keynesian position and it undeniably imposes limitations upon the analysis which others have been eager to exploit.

Consider, for example, Keynesian interest theory. Keynes posits that each individual will possess some expectation of a *normal* rate of interest which may diverge from the existing market rate of interest. If the norm one expects exceeds the market rate then this is tantamount to expecting market rates to rise in the future. In other words, one expects bond prices to fall and thus one sells bonds to hoard cash and avoid a capital loss. Suppose, however, that the market rate of interest does not rise – i.e. that bond prices do not fall. There is nothing in the theory which causes the individual to alter his opinion. He still retains the expectation that market rates will rise even after being proved incorrect for say, one, two or even five years. And all this time he is forgoing profitable investment in government bonds. In short, his expectation is not changed in the light of past experience and the observation that his concept of the normal rate has been shown to be incorrect. He does not *adapt* in the light of events.

Clearly this is a weakness of the underlying theory; what is required is some kind of *adaptive* mechanism whereby the rational utility-maximising individual will respond to the painful experience of being proved consistently wrong.

The feeling of dissatisfaction with the modelling of expectations formation in the *General Theory* was reinforced by developments in business cycle theory. Stated simply, it was felt that a purely psychological explanation of the business cycle was inadequate and that there were more fundamental forces at work. The missing link was to be provided by Paul Samuelson in his seminal essay (Samuelson, 1939) which combined interactions between the multiplier and the accelerator and laid the basis for all subsequent business cycle theorising. Together with this downgrading of the overriding importance of expectations, there developed a feeling that expectations should be capable of an endogenous explanation, in part because they should reflect the machinations inherent in the multiplier–accelerator analysis.

One of the earliest attempts to model expectations endogenously was undertaken by Metzler (1941). Again, the pivotal concern was with the business cycle, although in this pioneering article Metzler restricted himself to inventory cycles. Essentially, the underlying idea is that expected values are related to past experienced values on the one hand, but also to their recent trend on the other. Such expectations may be termed extrapolative in character. The great virtue of extrapolative expectations is that they can lend themselves to the prediction of cyclical movements. All that is required is a negative expectations coefficient on the trend variable to produce precisely the type of fluctuations mirrored in multiplier–accelerator analysis.

None the less, extrapolative expectations are essentially mechanical and, in particular, whilst they are linked to past observed trends, they are unrelated to past expectations and to past expectational errors. Economic agents are assumed not to respond to the fact that their expectations have been shown to be wrong in the past. It was with this crucial point that the expectations revolution in macroeconomics sought to deal. The idea that economic agents learn from past experience is crucial to the modern view of expectations formation. In the adaptive expectations approach, agents are assumed to learn from their past expectational mistakes. In the more extreme rational expectations philosophy they also learn with the passage of time about the true model governing the progress of the economy. Both approaches are generally critical of Keynesian economics and to this extent may be seen as part and parcel of the monetarist counter-revolution seeking to deny the Keynesian heresy.

Thus, the adaptive expectations approach sought to demonstrate that Keynesian interventionist policies would have only short-lived effects whilst the more extreme rational expectations approach leads to a logical denial of any effects at all in its more extreme versions. In doing so both approaches displayed considerable sophistication and technical skill which carried added conviction for many sceptics involved in the debate. None the less, it is perhaps well to note a subtle and far-reaching change in the approach to expectations theorising which possibly carries us away from the more fundamental concerns of Keynes. Although still carrying considerable implications for the business cycle, modern expectations theory is almost exclusively concerned with forming expectations over future prices, and in this regard it incorporated a comparatively simple quantity theory view of price determination. Fiscal policy changes are of significance primarily because of their monetary impacts. The output consequences of a collapse in over-optimistic expectations, which so occupied Keynes, is no longer part of the theory of expectations *per se* but rather a consequence of that theory combined with a host of other assumptions embodying what has become known as the New Classical Macroeconomics.

ADAPTIVE EXPECTATIONS

It is significant that adaptive expectations first made their appearance in the volume edited by Friedman (1956) heralding the reformulation of the Quantity Theory and initiating the monetarist counter-revolution, for much of the monetarist criticism of Keynesian and post-Keynesian economics relies heavily on the notion of adaptive expectations. Stated simply, adaptive expectations asserts that economic agents will revise their expectations in a predictable manner in the light of the extent that their prior expectations have been shown to be correct. More formally, if P* is the expected price level and P the actual price level, then where the subscript denotes the time period, we have

$$P^*_{t+1} = P^*_t + \alpha(P_t - P^*_t); \quad (0 < \alpha < 1) \qquad (5.1)$$

where α is the expectations coefficient. Thus the price level expected next period is equated with the price level expected this period *plus* some fraction of the extent to which that expectation was proved false. It follows that expectations are determined endogenously within the model and by reference to expectations held in all prior periods. None the less, as long as α is less than one, the influence of the more distant periods wanes geometrically and to all intents and purposes the influence of far distant expectations may be discounted entirely.

The adaptive expectations approach has great appeal. It is a comparatively simple means of modelling expectations and it is based on a model of behaviour which appears eminently sensible and in keeping with empirical observation, namely that individuals learn from past mistakes and grant greater weight to more recent experiences. Moreover, in the case of a once-and-for-all shock or disturbance, which pushes the economy from one steady-state equilibrium to another, it performs tolerably well. Suppose, for example, that the economy had enjoyed a stable price level over a protracted period of time, then the prevailing price level would be that expected. If now some exogenous disturbance, say an OPEC oil price shock, generates a sudden raising of the price level to a new equilibrium, the process of adaptive expectations will tend towards a new coincidence between the actual price level and expected price level in a reasonable period of time.[2]

The adaptive expectations mechanism underpins much of

2 The time-period of adjustment depends upon the value taken by α. If α equals one the adjustment is complete within one period. This is the assumption underlying the Cobweb theorem of price determination.

the monetarist assault upon Keynesian aggregate demand strategies. In particular, it questions the permanence of the trade-off between unemployment and inflation depicted in the negatively-sloped Phillips curve. In so doing, it establishes the basis of the concept of the 'natural' level of unemployment implicit in the notion of the vertical long-run aggregate supply curve.

To develop this issue in more detail consider Figure 5.1. Assume initially we have the combination $OQ_1 OP_1$ determined by the negatively-sloped aggregate demand curve AD^1 and the positively-sloped short-run aggregate supply curve AS^1. Assume now a raising of the level of aggregate demand to AD^2 raising output to OQ_2 and prices to OP_2 – a movement from A–B. The rise in prices erodes the real value of labour's wage and at the termination of the formal contract period labour will renegotiate for a higher nominal wage, raising marginal costs. As costs rise so too will the aggregate supply curve be shifted inwards, as indicated by AS^2, and ultimately the natural output level is regained at OQ_1 combined with the higher price level

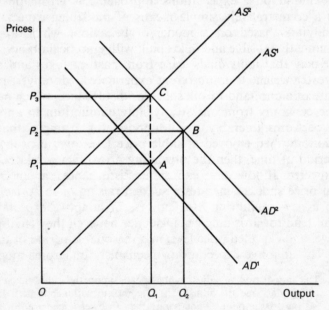

Figure 5.1 The adaptive adjustment mechanism

OP_2. The total movement, therefore, is from A → B → C implying that the long-run aggregate supply curve AS* is vertical above OQ_1 and implying only a limited scope for interventionist Keynesian demand management strategies.

The adaptive expectations approach has many advocates partly because of its simplicity for modelling purposes. None the less, it is not without its critics. As a means of expectations formation it performs badly in periods of accelerating inflation as a moment's reflection will amply demonstrate. It is not mere coincidence that dissatisfaction with this approach came to a head with the spiralling inflation of the 1970s. Further, it generates expectational errors which are systematically biased.

Implicit in our preceding illustration, for example, labour's expectational error with respect to future inflation is always to its disadvantage. Above all, however, it stands in conflict with the very concept of *homo economicus* in that it postulates behaviour which is non-utility-maximising. It is this feature which offends the purist and it follows on the fact that it is a mode of expectations formation which is entirely backward-looking. That is to say that in the formation of expectations of the future, it ignores the facts of the current situation no matter how pertinent they may appear to be. To this extent, it must be discredited as being methodologically unsound.

It is for these reasons that the adaptive expectations approach has been substantially, if not entirely, superseded in macroeconomic theorising by the more seductive rational expectations approach. And the latter has generated even more radical implications for the scope of policy intervention which can only be described as anti-Keynesian in spirit. As such, they have been remarkably in keeping with the non-interventionist philosophy and ideology prevailing on both sides of the Atlantic in recent years.

RATIONAL EXPECTATIONS

The concept of rational expectations was introduced into economics by Muth (1961) essentially in a microeconomic context but it was not until the 1970s that its startling macroeconomic policy conclusions were derived. Today, the rational expectations revolution combined with the ideas emanating from the New Classical Macroeconomics have coalesced into an extreme form of monetarism, which may be viewed both as an extension and a critique of the adaptive expectations approach, and which leads to an emphatic rejection of Keynesian-oriented interventionist policies even in the short term. Although the extreme version of this non-interventionist philosophy has been increasingly called into question, leading to a certain distancing of the rational expectations hypothesis away from the New Classical Macroeconomics, it none the less conveys the flavour of the more important policy debates and has been instrumental, if only indirectly, in providing the provisional justification for the consideration of supply side economics.

The reason for the application of rational expectations to macroeconomics is not hard to find. It derives partly from the sad state in which macroeconomic theory found itself in the early 1970s, with the phenomenon of stagflation confounding earlier Keynesian optimism and with the Phillips curve apparently experiencing increasing instability and collapse. It also relates to the fact that the adaptive expectations thesis associated closely with the name of Cagan (1956), which had allowed expectations to be modelled successfully in the relatively stable price era of the 1950s and 1960s, became increasingly untenable as a model of expectations formation under conditions of accelerating inflation which typified the 1970s. In addition, parallel developments in General Equilibrium Theory, and in particular the Arrow–Debreu achievements in Walrasian general equilibrium, carried implications for macroeconomics and reinforced the growing awareness that macroeconomic relationships must possess microeconomic foundations which assume utility-maximising behaviour. All these factors coalesced in suggesting that the rational expectations hypothesis might be usefully integrated into a macroeconomic framework.

The rational expectations thesis comes in strong and weak guises. The latter amounts to no more than a rather bland assertion that in forming expectations about the future economic agents will take into account not only the past record but also any additional current information should it appear worthwhile to do so. That is to say, that current information will be incorporated into the formation of expectations if it appears that the potential benefits of doing so outweigh any attendant costs. Since, in many cases, the cost of using current information is virtually zero (taking account of an announcement of a change in the policy regime, for example) whilst in others the benefits of using current information will be substantial (as in dealings with specialised financial markets, commodity markets, and so forth) it seems reasonable to posit that current information will be fully considered. For this reason alone, rational expectations must be considered superior to adaptive or extrapolative expectations formation which are purely backward-looking.

In its weak version the rational expectations thesis is not inconsistent with Keynesian economics. Keynes was fully aware that agents resort to current information; indeed, he is at pains to emphasise that the facts of the current situation often exert a disproportionate influence upon the expectation of future long-term yields – a factor making for prolongation of slump conditions.

Secondly, it is assumed that individual economic agents will process the information they find worthwhile to consider in an efficient manner in forming their expectations. In turn this demands a further assumption, namely, that economic agents will possess some conceptual understanding of how the economy actually operates – that they possess some form of economic model in deriving their expectations. Such an assumption also appears in strong and weak versions. In the latter case, it is not assumed that economic agents possess knowledge of a sophisticated structural equation model which *explains* the intricate workings of the macro-economy. Rather, it is assumed, relying on past experience, that they possess some form of *intuitive* reduced-form approach to economic modelling to permit them to make reasonably efficient predictions.

However, whilst it is the weak version of the thesis which is often invoked to justify the almost self-evident reasonableness of the doctrine, it is the far more stringent Muthian version which is responsible for the denial and dismissal of Keynesianism as a relevant policy document. The Muthian statement is completely at variance with the 'animal spirits' approach of Keynes. First and foremost, the world is viewed almost entirely in probabilistic terms. Uncertainty, in the Keynesian sense, is abolished. Outcomes have *objective* probability distributions as well as mathematically well-defined mean values. Moreover, individual economic agents are not only possessed with intelligence but also with the ability to perceive ultimately, via a learning process, the true model governing the economy. This is the crux of rational expectations; they are perceived as being *informed predictions* of future events and as such are essentially the same as the predictions of the relevant economic theory. Economc agents will thus form subjective expectations concerning future economic variables whose mean value will coincide with the true mathematical objective conditional expectation to be taken by those variables. An even stronger proposition pertains, first broached in Muth (1961), namely that not only do we have a coincidence of objective and subjective mean values but also that it is possible to have a coincidence between the agents' subjective probability distribution of all possible outcomes and the actual objective distribution pertaining in fact. The implication is clear; not only do agents possess a structural equation model of the economy describing the functional relationships involved but they also possess knowledge of the structural parameters involved. Nothing could be more removed from the world of Keynes.

This extreme version of rational expectations does permit of uncertainty, although not in the sense of Keynes. It allows for uncertainty in the sense that the world is not entirely predictable. In the absence of uncertainty the doctrine would be tantamount to having perfect foresight. Thus outcomes may occur which depart from expected mean values. But any such forecast errors will be totally random and will themselves possess the characteristic that the conditional expectation of the forecast error was zero. Moreover, any forecast error will be completely uncorrelated with any available information considered worthwhile to analyse, since, if any correlation existed, it would have been taken account of in forming the initial expectation. Implicit in this statement is the belief that economic agents will not make systematic errors; such errors can only occur because the learning process of the true model is incomplete. But in the process of learning, such errors will be eliminated. In contrast to the adaptive expectations approach, any forecast errors which remain will be essentially random, will reveal no discernible pattern and will be possessed of a mean value of zero. Finally, the variance of such forecasting errors will be less than that associated with any other method of forecasting; it is in this sense that rational expectations ranks as the most efficient means of expectations formation.

The fundamental objection levied against rational expectations theory turns upon the ability of economic agents to acquire sufficient information to derive the correct model of the economy. What guarantee can there be that agents possessed of finite lives will ever generate sufficient information in an economy experiencing continuous structural change? Indeed, in an economy undergoing structural change, the elimination of systematic errors becomes more problematic. Implicitly, therefore, rational expectations theorists have perceived the world as following an ongoing process whose essential features constantly recur. Although no one situation ever precisely duplicates another, the scheme of interplay is such as to constitute an identifiable pattern. None the less, this still demands that economic agents are remarkably perceptive in their judgements, able to distinguish what is unique from that which is part and parcel of the ongoing process.

To bring this issue into perspective it is perhaps useful to consider an elementary example. In the repeated tossing of an unbiased die it seems reasonable to assume that sooner or later all individual agents will perceive the mathematically expected mean outcome – even though it is not a possible outcome – especially if they are made to suffer a financial penalty for expectational errors. Those agents aware of probability theory (i.e. possessed of the structural equation model) will immediately identify the mathematically expected mean. But even those unacquainted with the laws of chance will soon learn from the expensive process of making systematic mistakes. Ultimately then, all agents' subjective mean values will coincide with objective mathematically expected mean values and this condition might be regarded as a rational expectations equilibrium. It will be an optimal situation in the sense that it will minimise the financial penalties associated with expectational errors, since the variance of expectation error is itself minimised. Now it is precisely this type of behaviour which underlies rational expectations thinking with respect to the macro-economy. The question is whether it is really permissible to make such a transition. Two issues seem decidedly relevant in attempting to answer this question. First of all, even the relatively uninitiated can learn all there is to learn about the tossing of an unbiased die in a relatively short space of time. In consequence it is reasonable to assume that the learning process will be complete within the finite lifespan of the agent. For analytical purposes, the latter may be assumed infinite. However, this may not be the case with respect to the macro-economy. Secondly, it will be appreciated that the very issue of structural change is absent in the die tossing experiment. The probability distribution is fixed and unchanging; there is consequently no impediment to retard or prevent the learning process; the coincidence of subjective and objective mean values can only be a question of time. This is clearly not the case in the real world.[3] Finally, and in many respects the most compelling difference, is the fact that expectation errors in the die-throwing experiment do not impinge upon the eventual outcome. Again, this is crucial to the success of the learning process. Even the agent who starts out making the most widely inaccurate systematic errors with regard to the mathematically objective mean value, does not impinge upon the ultimately observed distribution. Now this assumption does not remain tenable with respect to the macro-economy. Expectational errors maintained in labour markets, for example, do impinge upon output and employment patterns. How, then, does the economic agent learn the true model governing the economy, unless he is already

---

3 Correspondence with the real-world situation would require, for example, that the die become progressively more and more biased towards a certain outcome as the die-tossing experiment continued. The question which then arises is whether individual agents have sufficient information to predict the change in the conditional probabilities as they arise.

aware of how his state of ignorance affects the observed outcome? – a qualification, it may be noted, which is tantamount to a denial of ignorance in the first instance. How valid is the analogy between partial equilibrium settings possessed of purely probabilistically determined outcomes with the enormous complexities of the general equilibrium model of the real world?

We have dwelt at some length on the nature of rational expectations mainly because of its current dominance in the macroeconomic literature and because it is fundamental to many of the conclusions arising out of the New Classical Macroeconomics. As always, however, our primary concern is with the macroeconomic policy implications and their relationship with Keynesian economics. This will be the focal point of the following chapter. However, it is perhaps instructive to indicate the flavour of the argument in terms of Figure 5.1 which we have already employed. The objection that the rational expectations theorist might raise to the adaptive adjustment mechanism employed there would probably be along the following lines. Why should intelligent human beings, concerned with utility-maximising behaviour, actually wait until their real earnings have declined before embarking on corrective action? Will they not learn, in the light of past experience, to anticipate the consequences of government policies? Indeed, if governments follow fairly predictable countercyclical policies, will not intelligent beings learn to predict the policies themselves? In terms of Figure 5.1, what this implies is that as soon as the change in policy is announced, or more extremely, as soon as the change in policy is anticipated, then trade unions will immediately respond so as to defend their real living standards. In doing so, they will effectively negate the impact of the macroeconomic demand management policy. By renegotiating a new nominal wage agreement to protect their living standards they will effect a movement from $A \rightarrow C$ without going through the intermediate stage represented by point B. The short-term trade-off disappears. Indeed, the distinction between the short and the long term to all intents and purposes disappears; we are now in a world of vertical Phillips curves and vertical aggregate supply curves regardless of the time dimension. The Keynesian policy prescription is denied.

6 New Classical Macroeconomics and the Supply-Side Strategy

INTRODUCTON

We have examined the concept of rational expectations as an alternative and arguably superior mode of expectations formation. We now wish to examine some of the policy implications in more detail and in so doing derive the essential core of the New Classical Economics. Before proceeding in this way, however, it is important to emphasise that the New Classical Macroeconomics, associated in particular with the names of Lucas, Barro, Wallace and Sargent, builds upon other crucial assumptions besides the doctrine of rational expectations. In particular, it tends to assume that market-clearing is the normal optimising condition in all markets, including labour markets, and that departures from the norm are due primarily to information failures. The conclusions derived from the New Classical Macroeconomics tend to be conservative in character and serve to minimise the role accorded to active interventionist policy along Keynesian lines. Accordingly, it is important to note that there are advocates of rational expectations formation who do not endorse the new classical position and who, because they emphasise the absence of market-clearing conditions, are able to reconcile rational expectations formation with essentially Keynesian-oriented interventionist policies.

NEW CLASSICAL MACROECONOMICS

The essential assumption underlying New Classical Macro-economics is the belief that markets continuously clear. In turn, this requires the assumption of almost unlimited price and wage flexibility, as implied in the Walrasian setting blessed by the presence of the benevolent auctioneer. Now the appeal of this general equilibrium approach derives from two distinct sources. On the one hand, it is contended that Keynesian disequilibrium models rely on a statement of price rigidities not adequately accounted for by any clear under-lying theoretical statement. Thus the entire Keynesian edifice and justification for interventionist policies rests, so it is alleged, on an as yet absent theory. Secondly, in the absence of such a theory to account for rational individuals choosing to depart from market-clearing behaviour, the assumption is tantamount to the adoption of non-utility-maximising behaviour. When markets fail to clear, that is when false trading occurs; it implies that some trading is not taking place even though it would be mutually advantageous to parties on both sides of the market. Both buyers and sellers are failing to exploit opportunities which directly improve welfare. In terms of Figure 6.1, if the market price/quantity combination is indicated as $\bar{P}\bar{Q}$, it implies that there are sellers perfectly willing to supply the additional amount $\bar{Q}-Q_1$ at prices ranging between P_2-P_1 whilst equally there are buyers willing to pay prices between $\bar{P}$ and P_1 to consume the extra amount $\bar{Q}-Q_1$.

Welfare is not being maximised and the shaded areas in the figure indicate the loss in consumers' and producers' surplus. Accordingly, we have a theory with microeconomic underpinnings to explain why markets should clear. We do not have, in the new classical view, a convincing explanation as to why supply should fail to equal demand.

This belief in market-clearing conditions is reinforced by a tendency to invoke models which assume a one-product

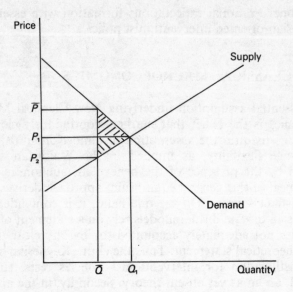

Figure 6.1 False trading and the loss of consumers' and producers' surplus

economy in which all producers are price-takers operating in competitive conditions. Under such conditions it becomes perfectly logical to analyse markets in terms of their being efficient auction markets which generate market-clearing conditions. In a market organised along the lines of a Walrasian auction, the assumption of market-clearing appears a reasonable one to make. And there is no doubt that certain markets readily lend themselves to such auction trading. When the product is sufficiently standardised and uniform to be homogeneous from the subjective vantage-point of the buyer, as in the case of certain financial markets and commodity markets, the potential buyer need not 'inspect' the product at all; he has all the information he needs, obtained most inexpensively, to make a rational decision, and he can then enter such a market through the services of a specialist agent or broker. Such markets will, accordingly, tend to be dominated by specialist traders, possessed of considerable stocks of the good in question, and it is reasonable to assume that such markets will operate very closely to the market-clearing price.

This conclusion rests on the fact that in such a market every trader will have the incentive to estimate both what the market-clearing price is ultimately going to be and also when such a price is going to occur. If he is possessed of such information he will be able to exploit his knowledge – either by buying or selling – to make abnormal profits. However, the same incentive will be open to all specialist traders; they too will have the time and effort and resources to generate and process the required information. Given the existence of competition, and in particular equal potential access to the relevant data, all specialist traders will tend to generate expectations of the market-clearing price which coincide within fairly narrow limits. In such conditions, actual prices will invariably be close to market-clearing prices. Accordingly, such markets, deemed 'efficient markets', are characterised by flexible prices; or, to use the term initially invoked by Hicks (1974), they are flexprice markets. The behaviour of specialist traders described above is, of course, entirely in keeping with rational expectations formulation. The only difference in their behaviour from that of the 'average' economic agent is that they find it worthwhile to collect and analyse a far greater volume of information. Indeed, the absence of sustained abnormal profits in such specialist markets is often invoked as evidence of rational expectations formation.

It is but a short step to assert that what is undeniably utility-maximising behaviour in specialist financial and commodity markets should logically be utility-maximising behaviour in any other market – hence the assertion that market-clearing is a generalised phenomenon throughout the economy, implying considerable general wage and price flexibility.

POLICY IMPLICATIONS

Let us assume that price-clearing markets are indeed the normal case. What implications follow in conjunction with the assumption of rational expectations formation?

The Policy Ineffectiveness Proposition

For reasons already outlined, if economic agents succeed in learning the true model of the economy they will be able to anticipate the effects of demand management strategies upon prices and quantities, and in seeking to protect their own real interest they will eliminate the output effects entirely. Thus, to all intents and purposes, the aggregate supply curve is vertical even in the short run so that any demand management strategy translates solely into price level changes. Now it may be objected that this result presupposes that economic agents can react with immediate effect to the demand management stimulus such that no lags are allowed to blunt their response. However, the rational expectations ineffectiveness proposition is even stronger than that stated above because, by implication, it suggests that rational economic agents will correctly anticipate the aggregate demand management strategy even *before* it is announced and put into effect. Thus, for example, if government countercyclical policy is systematic, in the sense that it is sensibly countercyclical, then rational economic agents will anticipate stimulatory policies when they perceive the economy moving into recession and equally will anticipate contractionary policies when the economy experiences boom conditions. They will thus co-ordinate their response to the policy measure long before it is effected, thus ensuring its ineffectiveness. The corollary of this proposition is perhaps even more daunting for the Keynesian-oriented economist because it suggests that completely non-systematic or nonsensical random countercyclical policy will have a macroeconomic impact simply because it will be incapable of being anticipated. It is hardly likely to be conducive to stabilisation goals however; nothing could so effectively sound the death knell for the concept of macroeconomic fine tuning. This policy ineffectiveness proposition refers to macroeconomic policy whether monetary or fiscal since the latter is seen primarily in monetarist terms as exerting its major impact upon the money supply operating through the economics of the budget constraint. This is not to deny that fiscal changes essentially of a *microeconomic* nature will exert real effects by influencing comparative prices and hence incentives.

The Cost of Eliminating Inflation

One of the most contentious issues which divides Keynesians and monetarists turns upon the costs involved, in terms of additional unemployment and output forgone, in the attempt to eliminate or substantially curtail the rate of inflation. Keynesians are prone to argue that the costs of deflationary policies will be substantial and long drawn-out and indeed are inclined to the view that it might be better to learn to live with moderate inflation. Monetarists, on the other hand, are more optimistic yet concede that output losses can be significant in the short term. Rational expectations theorists, however, are driven to the logical conclusion implicit in their thesis that the costs in principle should be minimal and the adjustment period decidedly short-term.

To bring out these respective positions in more detail let us have recourse to the aggregate supply and demand analysis employed in Figure 6.2. Here we assume an initial price output combination, OP_1OQ_1 determined by the intersection

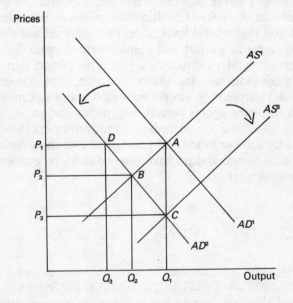

Figure 6.2 Alternative responses to deflationary policies

of the aggregate supply and demand schedules AS^1 and AD^1. For purposes of exposition let us assume that this initial output level also corresponds to the 'natural' level of output and unemployment. If the authorities now attempt to impose deflationary policies they will reduce the level of aggregate demand and thus generate the revised schedule AD^2. What are the consequences?

The Keynesians, emphasising the downward rigidity of prices, would stress that the entire adjustment would be thrown on the side of output and employment; prices would remain at the level OP_1 and output would fall by the extent A–D to OQ_3. In contrast, the conventional monetarists employing adaptive expectations formation would suggest that there would be an initial fall in both output and prices to OQ_2 and OP_2 respectively, implied by the movement $A \rightarrow B$. The fall in prices raises the real wage of those in employment. Renegotiation of the nominal wage consistent with regaining the original real wage pertaining to the natural level of output would imply a long-run outward shift of the aggregate supply curve to AS^2. Thus the monetarist views the sequence as $A \rightarrow B \rightarrow C$; ultimately a lower price level is attained and the natural level of output regained but there is a cost in terms of output and employment forgone in the interim period. And of course, this interim period can be quite long drawn-out. In sharp contrast, the rational expectations viewpoint is altogether much more optimistic. If utility-maximising agents perceive the policy and anticipate the consequences and act accordingly the movement $A \rightarrow C$ will be rapidly accomplished and the output and employment losses will be minimal and positive solely due to the existence of lags in adjustment.

DEVIATIONS FROM THE NATURAL RATE

Rational expectations combined with continuous market-clearing generates the logical proposition that the fluctuations in aggregate demand translate into price movements with output and employment levels unaltered. The natural level of output and employment remains constant and the business cycle becomes a purely nominal phenomenon. Now, such a scenario possesses one basic difficulty; it contradicts the actual experience witnessed in the real world. How then can the New Classical Macroeconomics explain observed deviations from the natural rate?

Essentially, deviations from the natural rate are to be explained in one of two ways. In the first case, they may arise from misperception. Economic agents may perceive a general price change as representing a relative price change. Thus, for example, suppose an increase occurs in the level of aggregate nominal demand financed by increased money supply, which generates, in accordance with classical microeconomic theory, a proportionate increase in all prices. The economic agent with perfect knowledge will be aware that all relative prices are unchanged. He will perceive that no change has occurred in any real variable, and in particular no change has occurred with respect to his real wage. Accordingly, he has no incentive to modify his supply of labour; employment remains unchanged and so does the volume of output. All that the nominal demand change can do is to alter the level of nominal prices; the money supply change is strictly neutral with respect to all real variables. In such a world, aggregate supply can only change if some fundamental change occurs in the underlying supply conditions. Thus, for example, technological change or innovation may shift the production function upwards for any given labour input; alternatively, in a dynamic context the supply of labour offered at any given wage may alter with population growth and so forth. None the less, the output level remains impervious to any demand stimuli.

However, once it is conceded that information may be costly and difficult to acquire and to process accurately, then it becomes possible for agents to form distorted impressions of general price changes. Agents will not normally enter all markets with the same frequency and therefore their knowledge of the less frequent markets will be subject to degenerative decay.

Moreover, there will be a time dimension to one's learning process concerning price changes. It is reasonable to assume, for example, that an economic agent will be immediately aware of a change in his nominal rate of pay (or perhaps in the rate of income taxation) which determines his nominal take-home pay, whereas he may need time to appreciate how other prices in more distant markets (less frequented markets) have also changed. Thus a distortion may be introduced into his perception of relative prices which may lead him to believe a change has occurred in his real wage and induce him to alter his supply of work effort. The economic agent's misspecification arises from the absence of complete and costless information; it does not arise from money illusion.

Let us illustrate this argument in more detail by assuming that the government causes an unanticipated increase in the money supply thus raising the level of aggregate demand. Let us continue to assume that all markets clear, implying that prices are perfectly flexible, but let us also assume that economic agents have imperfect information concerning prices prevailing in markets other than the one in which they trade. *Ceteris paribus*, the increase in nominal monetary demand will raise all prices equiproportionately. However, a seller finding an unexpectedly high price prevailing in *his* market may conclude that *relative* prices have changed in his favour. He may thus be induced to increase his output, unaware that his input costs have also risen, or, if he is a seller of labour services, to increase his supply of work effort, unaware of the increased price of consumption goods. Initially, therefore, there may be real output and employment effects in consequence of the money supply change. Precisely similar reasoning applies to a decrease in nominal aggregate demand occasioned by an unanticipated decrease in the money supply. Money supply changes are no longer neutral in their impacts. Of course, this process does not last indefinitely; sooner or later economic agents will learn about alternative price changes and thus obtain a truer perception of the change in relative prices; when this learning process is complete the economy will again be restored to its Walrasian full employment equilibrium. Implicit in the rational expectations thesis is the concept that the process of adjustment will not be aided by discretionary countercyclical macro-policy measures. Such measures will be anticipated and thus negated by the self-seeking actions of individual economic agents.

However, this explanation of the business cycle – rational expectational behaviour plus misperception – is not without certain conceptual problems, especially when the cyclical disturbance is prolonged over any significant period. One point in favour of the basic rational expectations hypothesis is that individual economic agents have wide access to inexpensive information services provided by the media, as well as enjoying the benefit of highly sophisticated specialist information services provided by membership of trade unions, trade associations and similar organisations enjoying enormous economies of scale in data collection and processing. Both wholesale and retail price indices are published not only with great frequency but, in addition, are accorded such prominence that it becomes virtually impossible not to acquire this information at zero cost. In a similar manner, it seems unrealistic to assume that economic agents will be misinformed about the real state of the labour market for any considerable period of time. If individual economic agents possess the learning ability required of them not to be misled by sophisticated yet systematic attempts at countercyclical policy imposed by the macro-authoritities, is it really sensible to assume that they will require much time to learn about the true state of the employment market?

The misperception thesis would be far more convincing if there were a significant time-lag existing between the decision to sell one's labour and the decision to buy consumption goods. In this event, one might reasonably infer a mistaken impression of the real wage. But in fact, most economic agents are sellers of labour and active consumers at the same time. In short, the theory of misperception appears inadequate to explain the duration of the cycle over a prolonged period of time.

Of course, it remains true that once made an output or employment decision cannot be reversed at zero cost. If a business firm, for example, mistakenly perceives a general price increase as being a relative price increase in its favour, which induces it to enlarge its capacity output by undertaking new investment, it will not normally pay to cancel the

investment altogether when the real truth dawns.[1] Optimal
strategy will probably suggest a continuation of the act of
investment most probably at a lower rate of implementation.
Thus, initial output effects may continue into subsequent
time-periods even when there is no real basis for their
existence. This is an important consideration which must be
given full allowance in considering departures from the
natural rate. Moreover, it meets an objection which has
frequently, if erroneously, been levied against the New Classical
Macroeconomics. It is sometimes claimed, for example, that
the logic of the rational expectation thesis requires that
deviations from the natural rate must be essentially random,
so that output will be higher than the natural level in one
period and lower in the next. It cannot explain, so it is alleged,
why output (and employment) remain persistently below the
natural rate for long periods of time in slump conditions
or equally remain persistently above for long periods in boom
conditions. In other words, rational expectations formation
should not generate serial correlation or 'persistence' in real
variables as displayed in the empirical evidence. In this
respect, adaptive expectations appears more compatible with
the data. However, this critique is essentially misleading since
it is perfectly possible for random and serially uncorrelated
forecast errors to generate results in real variables which
reveal serial correlation. A simple example is provided by
Blinder and Fischer (1981). An unexpected one-period
increase in aggregate demand occurring in period t will be
met, partially at least, by depleting inventories in period t.
Restoration of inventories to desired levels will then
necessitate increased production in subsequent time periods
at some optimally determined rate.

1 This type of misperception may be quite common in that a business
   unit will probably become aware of a change in the price of its final
   good before it becomes aware of similar changes in the price of its
   factor inputs – given the natural time lag inherent in the production
   period. However, it is difficult to pin substantial deviations from the
   natural rate upon such a phenomenon because the very logic of the
   rational expectations model would suggest that the firm learns by its
   experience to eliminate systematic errors. Thus, it should learn to expect
   that a change in the price of its final product may well be followed
   by similar changes in the price of its factor inputs.

A second cause of deviation from the natural rate is of course random shocks or events which could not have been sensibly anticipated by economic agents even allowing for rational expectations formation. Such random shocks include erratic and hence unpredictable actions on the part of the monetary authorities, which may generate price movements at variance with price movements which had been expected. In turn, this may reinforce or exaggerate the degree of confusion between general and relative price changes leading to output and employment variations. None the less, even allowing for the induced phenomenon of persistence, given the belief in market-clearing, it seems difficult to explain how such marked deviations from the natural rate could continue over such a prolonged period of time as witnessed in the post-war business cycles.

FURTHER IMPLICATIONS OF NEW CLASSICAL MACROECONOMICS

If deviations from the natural rate do derive from economic agents mistaking general price changes as relative price changes, then it would suggest that such misperceptions would be less likely, *ceteris paribus*, the more volatile the price level. In other words, one would expect the aggregate supply curve to be more vertical the greater the volatility of actual prices. This suggests a possible empirical test to establish the validity of the New Classical Economics but once again the results have been less than clear-cut and subject to different interpretations (Alberro, 1981). An alternative empirical approach has been suggested and attempted by Barro. Since the essence of the New Classical Economics rests on the belief that only unanticipated monetary changes will generate real effects, why not divide the money supply change into its anticipated and unanticipated components and regress them on movements of national income and prices? The anticipated component is that which rational economic agents could have reasonably expected in the light of all relevant information and past observations of government policy and its principal determinants would include the level of government spending and the extent of unemployment. Barro's investigations along these lines have generally been favourable to New Classical Economics (Barro, 1977, 1978; Barro and Rush, 1980) but his findings have not gone unchallenged and in particular have been denied by Mishkin (1982a and b) who argues that anticipated monetary changes do exert real effects and continue to do so over a considerable period of time.

Finally, it may be noted that the entire concept of rational expectations has led to a serious questioning of the validity of macroeconomic modelling. Although econometric models, largely Keynesian in design, performed tolerably well in the 1950s and 1960s their predictive and explanatory power collapsed quite dramatically during the stagflation era of the 1970s. One reason for their disappointing performance appeared to lie in changes in the values of the parameters governing the structural equations of the model. Now such a situation creates a dilemma of colossal dimensions for the econometric model-builder, for essentially his task is that of deriving coefficients from time-series data and regression analysis which he believes describes the constant structure of the economy. Indeed, the purpose of simulation exercises is to compare alternative policy measures by reference to the constant parameters. However, this entire procedure is challenged by the concept of rational expectations since it suggests that changes in the policy regime will change the manner in which individuals respond to the policy measure and the changed response may well incorporate a change in the underlying parameters. Imposing constant values on coefficients which are not invariant to the policy regime invalidates much of the earlier econometric modelling and this insight – the so-called Lucas critique, after Lucas (1976) – will doubtless remain as one of the more enduring contributions stemming from the rational expectations revolution.

The New Classical Economics and the rational expectations thesis has been of lasting value in questioning the over-optimistic leanings of early Keynesians. It has raised doubts about the efficacy of active interventionist policies by suggesting that intelligent economic agents can so modify their behaviour as to negate, or at least modify, the impact of countercyclical policies. It also suggests the very reasonable proposition that anticipated policy changes exert weaker real impacts than unanticipated changes. It has raised grave doubts about the validity of much econometric modelling characteristic of the days of the Keynesian ascendancy. Above all, however, it has generated an awareness that Keynesian-oriented non-market-clearing models require a firmer theoretical foundation grounded in utility-maximising behaviour along conventional microeconomic lines. For this reason, it has been responsible – just as the monetarist counter-revolution was responsible – for bringing forth a more sophisticated Keynesianism which is fully compatible with rational expectations behaviour.

THE EVOLUTION OF SUPPLY-SIDE STRATEGY

The reactions against Keynesianism, first in its monetarist guise and then more dramatically in its new classical format, paved the way for the assertion of supply side policies. Indeed, the evolution of the debate could perhaps be caricatured in terms of the progressive steepening of the aggregate supply curve. In early naive Keynesian models, the aggregate supply curve was looked on as being virtually perfectly elastic, at least until full employment output was attained, so that any demand stimulus will be translated in real output gains with zero price impact. More sophisticated Keynesian models depicted a trade-off between output and prices but still assumed real output and employment effects consequent upon demand management policies. Monetarist models *à la* Friedman allowed for trade-off benefits in the short term but postulated long-run vertical aggregate supply curves implying purely long-term nominal changes. Finally, the extreme New Classical Macroeconomics dispensed with the distinction between the long run and the short run. Aggregate supply curves were always vertical and demand management policies were incapable of having real effects. This caricature is depicted with the aid of the four quadrant diagram of Figure 6.3

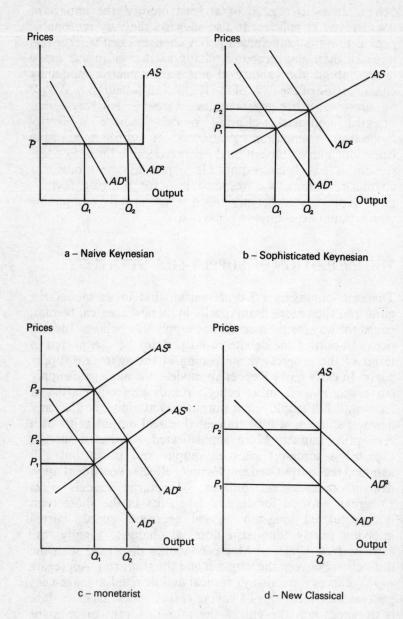

a – Naive Keynesian

b – Sophisticated Keynesian

c – monetarist

d – New Classical

Figure 6.3 The changing role of the aggregate supply curve

The assertion of the short-run vertical aggregate supply curve renders demand management policies irrelevant with respect to the real economy. The sole remaining role for demand management lies in deflationary monetary policies designed to curb or eliminate inflation. Such policies were often looked upon as a necessary prelude to the adoption of supply-side economics, the latter equated with microeconomic attempts to promote a favourable outward shift of the aggregate supply curve, raising the natural rate and economic growth. Thus was born the phenomenon of supply-side economics, the logical consequence of the denial of demand-determined Keynesian models and a reassertion of the classical message that supply creates its own demand. The adoption of such strategies was to be influential in dictating policies on both sides of the Atlantic. It was in the United Kingdom, however that these policies were promoted with almost religious zeal regardless of any attendant cost. We shall pay particular regard to the Thatcher experiment in Chapter 8. For the moment, we shall content ourselves with sketching the essential features of the supply-side philosophy as it applied in the UK.

TAXATION AND INCENTIVES

Of paramount importance to the supply-side strategy is the belief that both the suppliers of labour and the suppliers of venture capital are sensitive to a change in the rate of monetary remuneration and in particular are discouraged by high marginal income tax rates. Policies to change the composition of the tax burden in favour of indirect taxes at the expense of income taxes and in particular to reduce extremely high marginal rates of taxation on high income-earners are recommended in the belief that they will promote greater work effort and increased output. In a similar vein, policies to overcome the poverty trap whereby low income-earners who receive means-tested benefits are faced with extremely high marginal tax rates bordering on (or exceeding in odd cases) 100 per cent are also advocated as a means of encouraging greater work effort. The theoretical case that

income taxes are a disincentive rests upon extremely thin
ground since *a priori* the outcome must remain indeterminate
in that both income effects (in favour of work effort) and
substitution effects (in favour of greater leisure) are involved.
Nor is the empirical evidence very convincing. Many
employees have to all intents and purposes no say over the
amount of hours they work given that they choose to be
in employment and for the vast majority of upper income-
earners other motives than purely financial considerations
predominate. None the less, the belief that income taxation
is a disincentive and a preference for indirect taxation
(arguably more regressive) remain unshakeable tenets in
Conservative philosophy. The remarkable growth in the size
of the 'black economy' (about which there is general
agreement even if dispute remains over its extent) is sometimes
taken as evidence of the disincentive effects of income
taxation. This, however, is a most unconvincing argument.
The reason for the popularity of the 'black economy' on
the consumer's side is that prices are lower, reflecting the
lower rate of pay of workers employed therein. Moreover,
it would seem that much of the appeal of the 'black economy'
resides in the evasion of VAT.

When considering the disincentive effects of taxation
mention should also be made of the possible disincentive
effects of unemployment benefits. Indeed, such benefits may
be considered as formally equivalent to a negative tax imposed
on the unemployed. It represents a subsidy to idleness in
the eyes of the more extreme right-wing viewpoints.
Consequently, certain supply-siders have advocated a
reduction in the rate of such benefits to provide an additional
incentive to work. However, such a remedy would appear
especially callous in the UK context where the replacement
ratio (the ratio of benefit to average earnings) is often
considerably lower than elsewhere and where unemployment
is often the consequence of deflationary monetarist policies
on the one hand, and secular regional decline on the other.

A much more intellectually respectable argument recently
advanced in the UK debate concerns the feasibility of
adopting the American experience of 'Workfare'. Under such
schemes, unemployed workers, whilst allowed time off to

engage in job search and so forth, are none the less required to provide a number of hours work per week in activities deemed beneficial to the community in order to continue to receive unemployment benefit. Advocates of such proposals point to the self-esteem enjoyed by the previously unemployed on being able to contribute useful service and also to the benefits obtained by having services provided at zero marginal cost. Both these propositions are at best dubious. Certaintly, self-esteem does not figure very prominently in the performance of the very menial jobs. Secondly, the cost of organisation, administration and the provision of materials is not inconsiderable as a recent study by Burton adequately testifies (Burton, 1987). To this extent it may be regarded as a Keynesian demand management measure directed at activities slightly more useful than pyramid-building. The primary theoretical argument in favour of Workfare is that it leads to an increase in the supply of labour causing wage rates to fall, thus extending the demand and promoting employment. This is because the recipients of unemployment benefits may not consider it worthwhile (quite rationally) to enter the labour market for, say, forty hours a week and end up with only slighly more than they currently enjoy, when due allowance is given to the costs involved in working, including travel, clothing, canteen meals, etc. If, however, they are compelled to offer forty hours of work anyway, in order to continue to receive compensation, then their willingness will be all the greater and they will voluntarily enter the labour market. If the equilibrium wage rate declines in consequence, again implying market-clearing behaviour, then the net impact upon the natural level of output and employment will be determined by the elasticity of demand for wage labour.

PRIVATISATION

A second plank of the new philosophy rests on the belief that the private sector is inherently more efficient than the public sector. Initially, this belief rested on the premise that the private sector confronts competition from which the public sector is often shielded by state-created monopoly powers. Competition is deemed beneficial in that it responds automatically to the changing composition of demand and ensures the provision of goods and services at the lowest possible economic cost. Above all, in responding to the price signals of the competitive market, information is generated without invoking the bureaucratic functioning of civil servants and politicians. Privatisation has three distinct elements. First, denationalisation – the outright sale of public sector assets to private shareholders; secondly, deregulation – the opening of state activities to private sector competition; and finally tendering, whereby public provision is contracted out to private firms via a system of franchising. In the process, it is argued, consumers will enjoy a superior service and will also benefit from an enlarged freedom of choice. Again, the essence is a belief in the virtues of the market economy as an efficient allocator of scarce resources.

In the United Kingdom, under the Thatcher regime, privatisation has been pushed to unprecedented limits and has been extended to areas of natural monopolies where competition is impractical and would be inefficient. Here, however, it is still contended that privatisation is conducive to efficiency because of shareholders' pressures upon management and because of the need to submit to greater financial scrutiny from the private banking sector when raising finance. Again, however, the evidence is far from convincing that privatisation without enhanced competition adds to performance (Millward, 1986) and in the UK case, the initial experience following the privatisation of British Telecom did not noticeably endear itself to the British consumer. It is, of course, with regard to the natural monopolies that the proceeds from the sale of public sector assets will be most significant, a consideration which has led many cynics to suggest that the real reason for their sale is not related to efficiency gains, but rather stems from the appeal of allowing short-term electioneering tax concessions. Whether a further ulterior motive resides in the belief that privatisation will make for the improved prospects of public sector wage settlements remains as yet unproven.

REDUCING LABOUR COSTS

Supply-side economics places the onus of high levels of natural unemployment on the shoulders of the trade unions in maintaining excessively high wages and pricing themselves out of potential markets. Consequently, part and parcel of the new philosophy is weakening the powers of the trade unions and promoting greater wage flexibility and dispensing with restrictions in job practices. The reduction in trade union powers is linked with attempts to promote greater union democracy by financing secret ballots before strike action can be called and limiting secondary picketing during strike action. At the same time, the attempt is made to condition wage expectations to what supply-siders consider more realistic levels. Part of the idea underlying youth training schemes, for example, is geared to creating the willingness to accept lower-paying jobs. In a similar vein, the powers of certain wage councils able to stipulate minimum rates of pay have been substantially curtailed whilst subsidies have been granted to the employers of lower-paid workers. Hand in hand with measures to promote wage flexibility are measures to encourage greater occupational and regional labour mobility. It is recognised, for example, that one factor exacerbating regional unemployment is the enormous disparity in the cost of housing between the North and the South.

Throughout the entire statement of supply-side strategy there runs the fervent belief in the virtue of competition and the efficiency of the market. Barriers to competition must be dismantled if welfare is to be enhanced. This doctrine, so much in keeping with the tenet of New Classicism, is maintained as an almost self-evident proposition. And with all self-evident truths, there is no need to invoke supporting evidence. It remains a matter of faith for good or for ill.

7 The Keynesian Response

INTRODUCTION

Traditional Keynesian analysis rested upon the notion of non-clearing behaviour, especially in labour markets, with no inherent tendency for any automatic adjustment. Although this viewpoint possessed the convenient property of appearing to be in accord with the observed facts' and evidence, particularly during the Great Depression, it was not, for all that, without certain drawbacks. First and foremost it lacked a micro-theoretic foundation deemed consistent with utility-maximising behaviour. Secondly, the conventional Keynesian analysis grounded in short-run nominal wage rigidity, exhibited a decidedly asymmetric appearance in that dis-equilibrium situations were characterised by labour being displaced from its supply curve whilst business firms remained firmly fixed on their labour demand curves at all points in time. Although this dichotomy in behaviour was perhaps consistent with the Keynesian reference to money illusion on behalf of workers, it was clearly less than satisfactory to assume that firms' behaviour would be so different from that of efficiently organised labour unions. Finally, the basic Keynesian model possessed one other fundamental difficulty in that it assumed that declining real wages typified an expanding economy, and conversely, that the real wage rate would rise as the economy moved into a slump. Now of course, the inverse relationship between real wages and employment followed naturally upon the classical assumptions of diminishing returns to labour input and payment in accordance with marginal productivity, both of which Keynes fully endorsed. Indeed, Keynes and the classical economists were in full agreement about one feature of the macroeconomy – namely, that increased employment required a reduction in the real wage rate. Unfortunately for both Keynesian and classical models, such an inverse relationship appeared inconsistent with the empirical evidence.

To bring out some of these points, it is perhaps instructive to have recourse to Figure 7.1. In part (a) of the composite figure we show the supply and demand for labour as a function of the real wage, whilst in part (b) we have the corresponding aggregate supply and demand schedules. Let us assume an initial position of equilibrium determined by the aggregate supply and demand schedules AS^1 and AD^1 implying the price output combination P_1Q_1. With a fixed nominal wage indicated by W_0 and the price level P_1, we have the real wage W_0/P_1 and the equilibrium employment level ON_1. Now let us posit a decrease in the level of aggregate

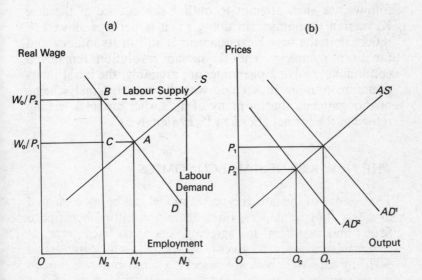

Figure 7.1 Unemployment in the traditional Keynesian model

demand, for whatever reason, indicated by a shift of the aggregate demand curve to AD^2. In this Keynesian world, what are the consequences? Initially, output contracts to OQ_2 whilst prices fall to OP_2. With a fixed nominal wage W_0; employment and real wages are thus inversely related. Labour is thus forced off its supply schedule (a movement from $A \rightarrow B$) but no such departure occurs for the firm in respect of its demand schedule. Finally, it may be noted that the level of unemployment which results is not just the difference between ON_1 and ON_2 for the rise in real wages induces a greater willingness to seek employment. The degree of involuntary unemployment is thus indicated by the amount $ON_3 - ON_2$.

The New Classical Macroeconomics combined with the doctrine of rational expectations has forced Keynesians to come to terms with the basic deficiencies of the elementary model. Just as the monetarist counter-revolution compelled Keynesians to take note of the importance of the budget constraint, and modify their analysis and policy recommendations accordingly, so too with the more extreme brand of monetarism combined with market-clearing. In what follows, we shall attempt to outline the essence of the new Keynesian economics. In doing so, it is perhaps as well to reflect that the new Keynesianism is still in its infancy and far from complete. The Keynesian revolution remains a continually evolving phenomenon; arguably, the latest interpretation is more in keeping with Keynes' original scheme of thought than that of many of his earlier disciples seeking refuge in the formal Hicksian IS/LM analysis.

THE NEW KEYNESIAN ECONOMICS

The essence of the new Keynesian model can be encapsulated in a few short sentences. First, there are mutual benefits to firms and workers in agreeing upon a fixed rate of remuneration over a given time-period which render it perfectly consistent with utility seeking behaviour even though it may impose external costs upon other sectors of the economy. Secondly, given that rational pricing policy often dictates the practice of mark-up pricing, whereby prices are related to average costs by a given percentage mark-up, and given that wages are often a major element in total costs, then the fact of fixed wage rates will often imply relatively fixed prices. Thirdly, if prices and wages are both fixed, at least over the immediate time-horizon, then changes in aggregate demand will be translated solely into changes in output and employment implying, *inter alia*, the provisional justification for Keynesian-oriented interventionist policies. Moreover, if wages and prices are both constant, then it follows that a movement from equilibrium will leave the real wage rate unchanged with simultaneous departures from both the firm's labour demand schedule and labour's labour supply schedule. Thus the asymmetry problem is neatly dispensed with. Moreover, with constant wages and prices, the division of aggregate demand changes into anticipated and unanticipated changes becomes irrelevant to the eventual outcome. Finally, there is no suggestion that real wages *must* fall in the upswing of the cycle or rise in the downswing; rather the analysis points to a comparative constancy in the real wage rate. We shall examine each of these propositions in more detail.

Wage Rigidity

When labour markets fail to clear, when wages are too high, it implies that there are some people who are unemployed who would in principle be willing to work for less than the going wage. Why, then, do firms not take advantage of this situation and cut the prevailing wage? There are doubtless all sorts of social and cultural influences that could be invoked in providing an answer to this question. Equally, however, it has been argued that the reluctance to cut existing wages can be explained purely in financial profit-maximising terms. This is what has become known as the *Efficiency Wage Hypothesis* – the notion that there is a level of wage payment which maximises profits because labour productivity is directly related to the wage paid. Of course, the level of the efficiency wage may itself depend upon prevailing economic conditions; it need not imply perfectly rigid wages. None the less, it is sufficient to suggest that wages need not fall to market-clearing levels; the firm does not have the incentive to reduce labour's productivity. The question which remains is why should labour productivity be related to the real wage paid by the business firm? Three distinct micro-economic rationales may be advanced in answer to this question (cf. Yellen, 1984).

Models of decreased shirking.

Such models, of which there are now several, possess two essential elements. First, the assumption that most workers possess some element of discretion in how well they perform their specified job and may therefore opt to diminish their work effort, and secondly, that shirking involves a risk, namely the possibility of detection and being sacked. If full employment prevailed throughout the economy, the deterrent cost of shirking would be eliminated for the sacked worker could then find similar employment elsewhere. Equilibrium thus requires all firms to raise wages above the market-clearing wage, implying unemployment and increasing the cost associated with job loss. Higher than market-clearing wage rates enhance labour productivity by providing incentives to reduced shirking. Higher than market-clearing wage levels thus act as a disciplinary device which may be reinforced by trade union pressures. The shirking model carries many implications. In particular, the existence of unemployment benefits reduces the potential cost of job loss due to shirking and the reduction is positively related to the replacement ratio. Such benefits may account for the observed secular decline in labour productivity in recent United States experience (see, for example, Weisskopf, Bowles and Gordon, 1984).

Reduced labour turnover.

Labour turnover is a costly process for the business firm. The payment of wages in excess of the going rate will diminish the incentive for existing labour to quit. Equally, in a general equilibrium context with all firms paying a wage in excess of the market clearing wage the presence of unemployment acts as a deterrent to quit the job. In a similar vein, incremental wage payments for seniority serve a similar purpose of retaining more experienced staff. The cost of labour turnover will, of course, differ between different firms and industry; none the less it explains why firms may choose to offer more than needed to attract potential employees.

Superior ability.
Since the workforce will be heterogeneous in respect of ability and general performance (where the latter may include any characteristic entering into the firm's preference function), the offer of higher than the market-clearing wages will permit the firm to be selective in its hiring policy and choose workers who conform to its perception of superior quality. Such considerations suggest that the firm has a positive interest in improving the average quality of its applicants since it perceives a direct relationship between 'quality' and profitability. This may be one explanation for the higher incidence of black as opposed to white unemployment if the former possess a lower reservation wage than the latter.

Efficiency wage theories explain why wages need not fall to market-clearing levels even in the face of extensive unemployment. Moreover, the efficiency wage model demonstrates wage interdependence between firms in that the optimal efficiency wage for any one firm depends upon the wage rate paid by competing firms. In such cases, and given uncertainty, it may be perfectly logical to leave wages unchanged even in the light of changes in the aggregate level of demand. Finally, it may be noticed that a more general explanation for wage rigidity has been advanced in the context of the efficiency wage model, to suggest that even when a change in wages may be indicated by reference to profit-maximising criteria, it may not be undertaken because the benefits of so doing are extremely small, even though the consequent loss imposed upon society may be large.

The Contract Period

A second major element of the New Keynesian model turns

upon the existence of long-term contracts freely entered into by both business firms and trade unions. Such long-term contractual agreements (often wholly or partially index-linked) exert an extended influence by modifying behaviour in the non-unionised sectors of the economy. In the United States in particular, where the majority of such contracts extend over a three-year period, the result serves to impart a sluggish response of nominal wages to changes in the level of aggregate demand. Thus aggregate demand impacts translate not into price changes via the medium of changing wage rates but rather into costly output and employment changes. In particular, a decline in the level of aggregate demand implies serious employment losses for the macro-economy. The question, then, is why should workers and firms voluntarily enter into such agreements in the first instance? The answer, in the simplest terms, is that such agreements confer benefits to both parties whilst the costs are borne externally by the macro-economy as a whole. It would be an extremely altruistic act, for example, for an employed worker to begin to renegotiate a downward reduction in his wage simply because he perceives an increase in the number of the unemployed.

What, then, are the benefits deriving from such long-term contractual agreements? For the business firm, the principal benefits arise from the fact that wage negotiations are a costly and time-consuming process and that the costs can be minimised by extending the period of contract. In addition, long-term contracts reduce the incidence of strikes. Similar advantages apply to the unions involved in lengthy wage negotiation procedures. For the individual workers, their willingness to accept a long-term wage agreement, even if it is not fully linked to the cost of living index[1] derives from the added security that such an agreement brings. Any decline in the real wage over the contract period can thus be likened

1 Although contracts fully indexed to the retail price index are not unknown they constitute a risk for the business firm in that it cannot guarantee that the price of its own product will keep pace with cost-of-living increases. This is particularly relevant to situations where living costs can be materially and dramatically influenced by external events, such as the OPEC oil price shocks of 1973/4 and 1979.

to an insurance premium that the worker pays in order to guarantee a given income over the period in question. Again, the reduced incidence of strikes deriving from long-term contracts is also perceived as a benefit for the majority of the workforce. We have already mentioned that formal contracts negotiated within the unionised sector will also provoke imitative behavior in the non-unionised sector. In addition, however, it is also the case that the latter sector may, for a host of cultural and sociological reasons, exhibit informal or implicit contracts which, although unspoken, none the less serve the same purpose of minimising the nominal wage response to changes in the prevailing level of aggregate demand. Such implicit contracts, 'the invisible handshake' in Okun's memorable phrase, may derive from paternalistic leanings of employers, the desire to maintain good public relations generally, or simply to conform with what is deemed to be the socially acceptable norm of behaviour.

PRICE STABILITY

The foregoing has suggested that it may be advantageous for firms to set wages above market-clearing levels on the one hand, and that it may be advantageous for both firms and trade unions to enter into long-term contractual agreements on the other. Both arguments point to stickiness in nominal wage rates despite changes in prevailing aggregate demand conditions. The question we pose now is simply, will comparative wage rigidity also imply comparative price rigidity? If so, it follows that changing demand patterns will reveal themselves in quantity adjustments, particularly upon the side of inventory changes, and ultimately such false trading will impinge upon employment levels as firms react to restore optimal inventory levels.

There are two distinct issues involved in a consideration of this question. First, the phenomenon of mark-up pricing is characteristic of many firms operating in oligopolistic and monopolistic market conditions. Its appeal lies primarily in its simplicity; it does not require sophisticated analysis at the senior management level before one can apply a percent-age mark-up above producer costs. Moreover, it is generally regarded as being fair in that business firms are seen to make price increases only when they are faced with an unavoidable rise in their production costs.

It follows automatically that if labour costs constitute a significant proportion of total costs then the combination of stable wage rates and mark-up pricing will make for a persistent tendency towards the maintenance of stable prices. Such behaviour upon the part of the business firm may be deemed perfectly rational given that there exist significant costs involved in making price changes. Indeed, in monopolistic markets, many firms will operate with fixed prices established over a broad range of unit cost conditions; only when costs diverge from the established range will the firm find it sensible to change its final product price.

Secondly, quite apart from the phenomenon of mark-up pricing, firms may find it convenient to enter into contractual arrangements to supply goods at a given price over a relatively protracted period of time. The arguments here are similar to those pertaining to contractual agreements between firms and trade unions. For the firm it has the benefit of reducing uncertainty and allowing the drawing up of optimal production plans; indeed, in many respects it may be looked upon as a natural corollary of having entered into long-term contractual arrangements to pay a given rate of wages over an extended production period. From the buyer's perspective, such agreements serve not only to ensure future supplies of essential materials but also they assist in reducing the costs associated with search activity. Even if future false trading is implied by such contractual arrangements the benefits to both parties may make it a perfectly sensible and rational trading relationship.

Again, even when contractual arrangements are absent, there are possible benefits to both buyer and seller in having prices predetermined and constant in the immediate period as opposed to their being determined in an auction-type market of Walrasian equilibrium. Such a distinction turns essentially upon the nature of the good itself. Auction sales can be applied to certain markets where the size of the transaction is large (a house, work of art, etc.) or where the physical presence of the buyer is not required (stocks, shares, commodity markets, etc.). For other commodities, and for small-scale transactions in consumer goods and services, an auction market would impose tremendous costs upon market participants – not least the cost of time and the inconvenience of attending a fixed location at a prescribed time. Price-fixing permits goods to be freely available at many locations at times convenient for the purchaser and on known terms which avoid the time-consuming auction process. As Gordon (1981) succinctly expresses it: 'The use of a price tag instead of a live trader or auctioneer can also be viewed as a substitution of cheap capital for expensive labor.' It is thus perfectly rational and sensible, as well as consistent with maximising behaviour, to announce fixed prices and to maintain them over lengthy periods, and there can be no doubt as a matter of empirical fact that many prices remain unchanged even over cyclical periods.

There are compelling reasons, then, why many prices will exhibit relative stability implying non-market-clearing behaviour on an extensive scale. With both money wages and prices constant, changing aggregate demand conditions reveal themselves in quantity and employment adjustments with *both* labour *and* the business firm being displaced from their respective supply and demand schedules. In terms of Figure 7.1, for example, where the decline in aggregate demand in part (b) of the composite figure implies the movement A → B in part (a), what is suggested by the revised Keynesian model is the movement A → C.

Of course, the Keynesian model outlined above is rather over-simplified in certain respects and can perhaps be considered as a caricature of the revised non-clearing model. In particular, the assumption of complete price inflexibility is rather extreme and does not allow for the fact that the prices of many intermediate inputs are indeed dependent upon markets conforming very closely with efficient auction market behaviour. Alternatively, in recessionary periods it is commonplace for business firms to grant often sizeable discounts (even though quoted prices remain unchanged) or to offer interest-free credit which in effect implies that percentage mark-ups are directly related to cyclical behaviour. Likewise, the assumption of complete wage inflexibility is again unnecessary and rather extreme. The concept of the efficiency wage is perfectly compatible with downward adjustment of nominal wages in recessionary periods. None the less, the New Keynesian economics does not depend upon strict wage and price inflexibility. After all, wages and prices did fall significantly during the Great Depression, although not enough to promote market-clearing. All it requires is that wages and prices are not sufficiently flexible or sufficiently responsive to be able to adjust to market-clearing levels, and in offering compelling reasons as to why this might indeed be the case, it provides a firmer theoretical basis to justify Keynesian interventionist policies. Given this framework, an autonomous decline in aggregate demand which would otherwise yield lost output and unemployment can be countered by discretionary demand management strategies.

Moreover, it is not commonly appreciated that when the assumption of perfect price flexibility is dropped, conventional Keynesian demand management policies may emerge in a more potent form *because of the assumptions inherent in the rational expectations thesis!* (Neary and Stiglitz, 1983.) In this analysis, the conventional New Classical Macroeconomic conclusion that fully anticipated government policy is ineffective has been seriously called into question. To illustrate, in a multi-period setting, an increase in government expenditure today possesses a spillover effect in raising national income at a future date. If this leads to the anticipation of an increased demand for labour at that future date, it will deplete the need for current savings and thus serve to raise the value of the multiplier in the current period. The wheel has turned full circle.

The revised New Keynesian model is still in the process of evolving. Its character will undoubtedly change in the course of the next ten years. It is in this sense that the Keynesian revolution, fifty years on, remains fluid and incomplete, constantly responding to its many critics by adopting greater sophistication and microeconomic rigour, and by dispensing with its earlier naivety and over-optimistic leanings. It none the less remains firmly in keeping with the spirit of Keynes in rejecting the belief that all is necessarily for the best in the best of all possible worlds.

8 The Thatcher Experiment and Reaganomics

INTRODUCTION

The year 1979 marked a watershed in British politics and in particular in the conduct of British post-war macro-economic policy. Prior to this date, British administrations, both Conservative and Labour, had pursued policies which could broadly be described as Keynesian in their orientation and which reflected a commitment to the idea of the 'mixed economy' in which the public sector played an important and often dominant role. This general consensus, sometimes labelled 'Butskellism' reflecting economic policy as expressed in the views of R. A. Butler, a former Conservative Chancellor of the Exchequer and Hugh Gaitskell, then leader of the Labour Party, dominated Treasury discussions and popular economic debate and has been admirably summarised by Burton (1981):

Specifically, the social democratic programme of all post-war Governments in Britain from the beginning of the Fifties until 1979 was for an admixture of Keynesian aggregate demand management, to stabilise the economy and provide full employment; an extensive 'welfare state', conducted by the provision of 'free' (i.e. zero-price but tax-financed) welfare services by government bureaucracies; income redistribution conducted by the provision of social security benefits to the poor, financed supposedly by high marginal rates of taxation at the other end of the income scale; the persistence (no great change either way) of the extensive volume of state ownership of industry in Britain; perennial attempts to cure inflation via incomes policies; ragged attempts to improve economic coordination by planning the economy *à la Française* (i.e. corporatist/indicative planning); acceptance and accommodation of the trade union movement as one of the 'great economic interests'; and extensive government financial intervention in 'private' industry via subsidies and government-sponsored mergers, to promote industrial efficiency and to solve 'regional' (often marginal constituency) problems. (p. 1)

Whilst this broad political programme had commanded wide acceptance during the 1950s and 1960s, the experience of the 1970s suggested that the patient was no longer responding to the recommended cure. Whereas interventionist demand management policies, primarily fiscal in their orientation, had *appeared* remarkably successful in promoting full employment with only modest inflation in the 1950s and 1960s, the decade of the 1970s witnessed the era of stagflation in which inflation and unemployment steadily increased together. To the dismay of Keynesians, the Phillips curve now appeared to have embarked on a progressive outward drift so that a time-series perspective of observed combinations of inflation rates and unemployment now traced out a positively inclined curve. Of course the difficulties were compounded by the four-fold increase in the price of oil in 1973/4 but the attempt to deal with this phenomenon by the adoption of prices and incomes policies was not marked by any notable success. The continued growth of the public sector did not appear to provide the answer to rising unemployment but rather served to generate increased bureaucracy in the public services, matched by a growing militancy on the part of the public sector unions, leading eventually to a wave of strikes generating widespread public hostility. This rising discontent reflecting the disquiet about inflation, trade union power, increased bureaucracy and heavy taxation was certainly instrumental in the advent of the Thatcher government in 1979. However, more important in determining the philosophy of the new administration was the intellectual revolution which immediately preceded it. The ascendant monetarism had directly questioned the wisdom of Keynesian interventionist policies and it was becoming increasingly influential in British academic circles. Although still reflecting a minority viewpoint, it was none the less a minority with an increasing audience and which was called upon for advice by Conservative Party leaders. Hand in hand with the monetarist revival went a renewed respect for the classical liberal tradition represented by the views of economists such as Milton Friedman, Friedrich Hayek and Alan Peacock. The academic exponent of the new philosophy in the Conservative Party was indisputably Sir Keith Joseph who was largely responsible for mapping out the new Conservative strategy in the period of opposition.

The transformation in economic policy heralded by the advent of the new government was dramatic. Previous administrations had relied upon demand management policies and concepts of 'fine tuning' to secure the goals of full employment and economic growth with the balance of payments deficit acting as the major, and on occasions overriding, constraint. The concern with inflation was a comparatively latterday phenomenon, explicable in part by the shock of the OPEC oil price rise and hence in principle of a transitory nature. This general leaning towards Keynesian-oriented policies was accompanied by a marked preference for fiscal as opposed to monetary control, reflecting the ease of making fiscal changes in the UK context, and also the distinct predilection of the Treasury whose formal model was decidedly Keynesian and until very recent times bereft of a monetary sector. Nothing could be more removed from the new doctrine.

BRITISH MONETARISM AND THE ROLE OF THE PSBR

Following the general election in 1979, all was changed. First and foremost, the control and ultimate elimination of *inflation took absolute priority*. This reflected not simply a difference in the ranking of competing policy goals determined by a subjective assessment of the relative costs of inflation and unemployment. Rather the control of inflation became regarded as the dominant objective because the *attainment of employment targets could not be achieved without it*. The economic rationale underlying this belief was not always clearly stated and appeared to rely on the assertion that inflation implied high interest rates, loss of international competitiveness (despite floating exchange rates) and created uncertainty inimical to investment spending. However, there was no doubt about the underlying message, namely, that unemployment was the consequence of preceding bouts of inflation triggered off (in many cases) by Keynesian-oriented attempts to raise the level of aggregate demand. Implicit in the new approach, therefore, lay a veiled critique of conventional Keynesianism and an acceptance of the natural rate hypothesis in that the latter was assumed invariant (in the long run at least) to aggregate demand stimulus.

If control of inflation is the overriding policy objective, then *control* of the money supply is the overriding policy instrument. Not only did the new Conservative government endorse a brand of monetarism but, in addition, they pursued a rather *simpliste* and mechanical quantity theory view of price determination. The money supply to be controlled was the relatively broadly defined £M3, a definition which included coins and notes in circulation plus bank deposits and served as a reasonably close proxy to immediate spending power. How was the money supply, so defined, to be controlled? In many respects, this was the most controversial question concerning the new orthodoxy. The answer stated simply rested on the belief that there was a reasonably stable and relatively clear-cut relationship between the £M3 definition of the money supply and the size of the Public Sector Borrowing Requirement (PSBR) which, loosely speaking, corresponded to the size of the government budget deficit. The relationship between the PSBR and the money supply was to be understood to refer to the medium term and it was claimed that it would hold regardless of the manner in which the public sector deficit was to be financed.[1]

---

1   That is, regardless of whether the deficit is financed by increasing the money supply or by bond sales to the non-bank private sector. In the latter case, bond sales would disturb the private sector's optimal portfolio balance between financial assets and money and the restoration of the latter would necessitate additional borrowing from the private banking sector.

Given that assertion, then the implications for fiscal policy are immense. If inflation is the number one policy objective to be controlled by control of the money supply, and if in turn the latter is to be controlled by control of the PSBR, then fiscal policy *per se* ceases to be an independent policy instrument. Levels of government expenditure and taxation are to be set so as to be consistent with the PSBR out-turn figure compatible with meeting the preannounced monetary supply targets. In brief, *fiscal policy becomes entirely subordinated to monetary considerations* in direct contrast to conventional Keynesian orthodoxy. The fiscal revolution is complete.

This was the essence of the Medium Term Financial Strategy (MTFS) – the subordination of fiscal policy to meet a purely nominal monetary target. In contrast to conventional Keynesian orthodoxy, fiscal policy was no longer to be directed towards the control of *real* variables. The new philosophy was to be summed up later by the Chancellor of the Exchequer, Nigel Lawson in the following terms (Mais Lecture, June 1984): 'It is the conquest of inflation, and not the pursuit of growth and employment, which is or should be the objective of macroeconomic policy.'

The most extreme example of this philosophy was to be demonstrated in the third budget of the new administration presented in March 1981 by Sir Geoffrey Howe, when in the attempt to steer the economy back to its monetarist/PSBR targeted course, massive tax increases were proposed at a time when the economy was already in deep recession, when all the relevant indicators were forecasting a severe deepening of the recession and when many private business firms were already faced with the daunting prospect of potential bankruptcy.

This emphasis on the size of the PSBR as the key economic benchmark reflected a return to a more elementary pre-Keynesian orthodoxy. Keynesian-oriented fiscal policy had stressed the importance of the *composition of the budget deficit*, arguing that expenditure changes were more high-powered than equivalent tax changes, that indirect taxes were more deflationary than direct taxes, and so forth. Now, with the *size of the PSBR* the focal point of attention, this sophistication was pushed firmly into the background, arguably with unfortunate results.

There were, of course, other facets of Conservative economic policy. Given the adoption of a decidedly monetarist stance, incomes policies, upon which previous administrations had relied, were dismissed as an irrelevancy. Indeed, non-interventionism became the order of the day. Competition and market forces were to be allowed free play and constraints upon trade were to be removed, for example, with the abolition of exchange controls.

One other aspect of the new policy was accorded importance. Great stress was attached to the role of expectations in conditioning the appropriate response from the private sector. Announcement of the target path of the PSBR would (assuming economic agents accepted the philosophy underlying the model analysis) generate correct expectations concerning the future rate of inflation – providing the target path was to be believed. The latter qualification is important because there can be no doubt that in the early days of the medium-term financial strategy, the enormous endogeneity displayed by the PSBR out-turn figures blew the policy off course and simultaneously destroyed credence in the ability of the authorities to control the money supply.

The incoming administration accepted that the policy would carry certain costs in the form of *increased unemployment*. This was looked upon as a necessary evil in the elimination of inflation and the creation of the foundations for future economic growth and prosperity. But it was believed that the adjustment process would be relatively swift, that unemployment would be contained within reasonable limits, and that a fitter, leaner and more efficient industrial structure would remain. This was probably the single most contentious issue arising from the fiscal and monetary policies of the new government; Keynesians and even moderate monetarists argued that the strict monetary targets then under discussion would inevitably generate severe output and unemployment losses especially given their interest rate and foreign exchange rate repercussions. The extreme monetarist stance of the new government, however, suggested a much more optimistic view; inflation would be brought under control in a relatively short period of time with relatively moderate losses in output and employment, and such losses as there were would be speedily regained in the new era of price stability.

In the event, the adjustment process was far more painful, traumatic and divisive than ever imagined. In the process of reducing inflation from approximately 10 per cent in May 1979 to approximately 4 per cent by the time of the general election of June 1983, unemployment climbed from some 1.2 million to in excess of 3 million. Yet despite the difficulties and setbacks the policy was pursued with an amazing consistency and almost religious zeal. Many commentators, including some relatively sympathetic to the new doctrine, suggested that the policy was operating under too stringent conditions and was perhaps pursuing the wrong definition of the money supply. Critics pointed to the undisputed overvaluation of sterling as an indicator of the excessive zeal with which the new policy was being pursued.

THE SUPPLY-SIDE STRATEGY

If control or the conquest of inflation was the first priority, to which macroeconomic policy was to be directed, the other side of the coin was represented by the supply-side strategy, which was to be the focal point of microeconomic policy. The macroeconomic elimination of inflation was thus viewed as a necessary ingredient to permit microeconomic policies to take effect. And the microeconomic policies were to be concerned not with prices as such, but rather with creating the conditions conducive to promoting a climate of enterprise in the interests of generating growth and employment. In short, the conventional micro/macro-policy dichotomy is turned on its head.

And it is the creation of conditions conducive to growth and employment, and not the suppression of price rises, which is or should be the objective of microeconomic policy. (Nigel Lawson, Mais Lecture, June 1984)

The new government argued that the economy would gradually attain its natural level of output and employment if left to its own devices and if the appropriate climate of competition were allowed to prevail. Important in this regard was the need to eliminate uncertainties, created by inflationary pressures, which could impede the natural adjustment process and interfere with the functioning of the market economy. In addition to the *passive* policy of allowing the economy to attain its natural rate, however, the government also firmly believed that it could pursue *active* discretionary policies to promote a raising of the natural rate. Such microeconomic policies were mainly concerned with providing incentives to greater work effort, enterprise and risk-taking. Tax changes were considered relevant solely to the extent that they impinged upon incentives and reinforced the supply-side strategy. Privatisation of substantial portions of the public sector was to be promoted to serve a dual purpose. On the one hand, it would lead to a raising of the natural rate since the private sector was intrinsically more efficient than bureaucratic government bodies, but in addition it was the means of financing substantial tax reductions without jeopardising the all-important money supply targets.

In addition to providing incentives, especially direct tax incentives, the other main means of encouraging the growth of output and employment lies in permitting the unfettered operation of free market forces. This aspect of policy is reflected in deregulation, the weakening of the powers of trade unions and other bodies possessed with restrictive powers (such as the wage councils) and ceasing to promote policies directed at combatting long-term structural change and regional decline. No longer is the attempt made to influence artificially the location of industry or to try to offset the secular decline of traditional industry which no longer enjoys a comparative advantage in international markets. The emergence of two nations – the impoverished North and the booming South-East–is seen not so much as a cause for concern as an inevitable consequence of market forces to which, sooner or later, rational economic agents will learn to adapt. And the concern expressed for the plight of the inner cities reflects a call for rejuvenation through the

promotion of new enterprise and the exploitation of new
opportunities and does not reflect in any sense a denial of
this basic tenet.

It was conceded that the supply-side policy, allowing for
the free play of market forces, would, inevitably, generate
not only regional disparities but would also make for greater
inequalities in general. Indeed, there is, and always has been,
a perceived trade-off between efficiency and equality. Such
a trade-off is fully allowed for in other political philosophies.
What is different about the new Conservative supply-side
strategy is its instinctive belief that society's collective social
welfare function favours efficiency over equality.[2]

Of course, it should not be assumed that these policies
were stated so categorically or were always so clearly
identified. Rather, this dual philosophy appeared to emerge
from a number of statements from government ministers and
Treasury officials which were not always commendable for
their clarity and precision. For example, on occasions, the
policy appeared to rest upon the reduction in the PSBR in
absolute terms; on others, the intermediate policy objective
is stated as one of achieving a reduction in the PSBR as
a percentage of GNP. Policy announcements were often
couched in cautious terms and subject to certain qualifications
and reservations – which politically speaking was no doubt
eminently sensible in the light of subsequent events. The
stringency with which the adopted policy was to be pursued
was also a matter of controversy within the Conservative
Party and indeed within the Cabinet itself. The latter, under
media pressure, was divided into hard-line monetarists on
the one hand, and more Keynesian-oriented 'Wets' on the
other. None the less, if the issues were not, in practice, as

2   That is to say, in terms of the indifference curve analysis of Figure
    8.1, the Thatcher view is that the tangency solution between the trade-off
    frontier and society's collective indifference curve occurs at point A
    as opposed to point B. The indifference curves are concave it will
    be noted, because both axes depict 'bads' as opposed to goods and
    the 'bliss point' coincides with the origin. In more dynamic terms,
    it is part and parcel of the new philosophy that the trade-off frontier
    is not immutable but may itself be changed by appropriate microecono-
    mic policies.

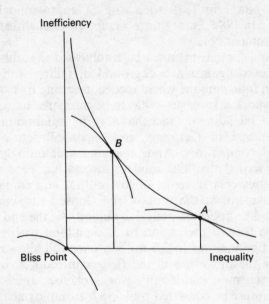

Figure 8.1 The efficiency–equality trade-off

clear-cut as outlined above, it is not a gross distortion to summarise the policy of the new administration as comprising a reduction in the money supply through control of the PSBR combined with an earnest belief in the power of supply-side economics.

EVALUATION – SUCCESS OR FAILURE?

It is beyond doubt that the Thatcher government pursued its dual policy with a single-mindedness that remains unique. Although the money supply targets have often been completely and hopelessly missed, and have also been redefined when an alternative measure appeared more convenient at the time, the general thrust of the policy has been maintained. The PSBR has been progressively reduced and in 1987 stood at less than 1 per cent of GDP. In the course of this development the rate of inflation fell from approximately 10 per cent at the time the administration came to power in 1979 to a rate of approximately 4.5% prevailing in 1987. Does this represent an unqualified success for government policy?

First and foremost it must be emphasised that this success was achieved against a background of falling world prices generally, following the world recession arising from the 1979 oil price shock. Moreover, it has to be compared to experience elsewhere, including the fact that *negative* inflation rates have been achieved in Germany and Japan, Britain's leading industrial competitors. And, even more dauntingly, it has to be conceded that this modest success has been attained at enormous cost in terms of lost output and employment. Unemployment, at the time of the Conservative victory in 1979 stood at approximately 1.2 million. At the end of 1987 the figure was in the region of 2.75 million with arguably the true figure closer to 3.5 million once full allowance was made for the distortion in the figures introduced by youth training schemes, community work schemes and so forth. Whilst it must be conceded that 1987 unemployment figures reflect a number of factors, not least the natural growth in the workforce, increasing labour productivity and the recession induced by the 1979 oil price crisis, there can be little doubt that they reveal the influence of an extremely strict monetarist stance which witnessed record interest rate levels and an exchange rate overvalued at one stage to an absurdly high $2.40 to the £. Deindustrialisation has continued, and the level of manufacturing prevailing in 1979 was regained only in 1987 after five years of uninterrupted growth. Import penetration has increased and Britain's share of world trade in manufacturing continues to decline. What is now being hailed as successful management of the economy would undoubtedly have been seen as a potentially disastrous outcome at the start of the experiment.

It is in the employment consequences of the monetarist policy and the failure to do anything for the resulting unemployment that the strongest charges must be levied at the Thatcher government's economic policy. Long-term Treasury forecasts for the foreseeable future point to a growth rate of the economy, which, together with projected growth rates for the labour supply and productivity, do not suggest any marked fall in the numbers of the unemployed. Moroever, the thrust of so much of present policy in relation to employment is directed predominantly to the creation of low-paying activities. Community work projects, youth training schemes and the abolition of wage councils do not reflect credit on the concept of an enterprise economy and inevitably increase the force of the poverty trap. For many critics, what is lacking is the failure to do anything concrete to promote a raising of aggregate demand. This is reflected in the decision to pursue tax-cutting programmes – consistently applied over successive Tory budgets – as opposed to promoting public expenditure programmes which carry a much greater initial demand impact. Tax cuts seep into savings and into imports – they promote 'jobs in Cologne and Tokyo' in the words of a former Labour Shadow Chancellor. Likewise, the abolition of exchange controls – an article of faith for a market-oriented administration – has seen a net outflow of venture capital at the rate of about £14 billion per year with net assets held overseas rising from some £12 billion to approximately £100 billion. Free marketeers would argue that venture capital should be free to seek the highest possible return, as being in the ultimate best interest, not only of the investor but of the country as well. However, this argument overlooks the social costs associated with unemployment and also the financial costs arising from social security expenditures and lost tax revenues.

What about the alleged gains to be recorded by the much-vaunted supply-side strategy? Lower tax rates, combined with the shift from direct to indirect taxation, reduced trade union powers culminating in the defeat of the miners' strike in 1985, the privatisation programme to promote efficiency, greater competition and market flexibility, all were intended to revitalise Britain's sluggish economy. What has in fact been achieved? That there have been productivity gains in certain areas, especially in small businesses, is not in dispute; equally a good deal of slack and overmanning has been eliminated in the new monetarist climate. It has to be conceded that the economy has witnessed an unprecedented growth in real output since 1982 – although such uninterrupted growth is to be explained partially from the abysmally low base (partly budget-induced) from which recovery began. Yet for many critics the impression remains that the greatest enterprise gains have been made in the progress of the black economy and little if anything has been achieved in respect of the level of wage settlements. Real earnings continue to run ahead of inflation for those fortunate to remain in employment and in consequence little progress has been made in conditioning wage expectations downwards. The supply-side strategy has all the appearance of an act of faith upon the part of its advocates to be pursued regardless of any conflicting evidence. Indeed, evidence does not figure very highly in the criteria invoked to determine policy. Nigel Lawson, for example, is on record as saying, 'I am not interested really in the arcane quibbles of econometricians'; followed by, 'the basic concept is very clear' – rather reminiscent of the man who demands 'don't confuse me with facts, I've made up my mind' (quoted by Currie, 1985). Certainly, there is little theoretical or empirical evidence to suggest that tax cuts are a panacea for Britain's economic malaise.

Finally, the question which must be asked is: how permanent are the gains associated with the progressive reduction in the PSBR as a percentage of GDP? The achievement was made possible partly by the autonomous growth of oil revenues from the development of North Sea oil which rose from a figure of £1 billion in 1979 to approximately £13 billion at its peak. But these revenues are now progressively declining as the oil-fields are being exhausted; Treasury estimates predict that they will yield less than £4 billion annually in the period following 1987. Similar considerations apply equally to the privatisation programme. The sale of national assets made a substantial input to the undershooting of PSBR targets in 1986 and 1987; revenues from such sales rose steadily from a level of £377 million in 1979 to over £2 billion annually by 1984/85 and further receipts are in the pipeline, partly from additional sales and partly because the purchase was staggered to accommodate the needs of small-scale investors (cf. Kay, Mayer and Thompson, 1986). But such sales are inevitably limited; there is a limit to the amount of stocks one can relinquish to finance day-to-day current expenditures. The analogy with selling the family silver is very real. Moreover, the sale of such assets has arguably worsened the prospects for the PSBR in future years. Short-term gains have to be set against the loss of future income from profitable state monopolies and arguably there is a net cost to the Exchequer involved because such sales have often been at a substantial discount well below true market values. The changing composition of the British population, the increasing dependency ratio and the demands of the old are also guaranteed to generate significant increases in public expenditures in future years. Underlying this concern, is the threat of the ever-present time-bomb posed by the State Earnings Related Pension Scheme (SERPS) which is grossly underfunded for future years and can only be honoured by the raising of substantial new revenues.

Nor are the prospects in the immediate short term particularly encouraging. The Treasury publishes a survey of medium-term forecasts made by outside observers and institutions, including academics and others. The consensus suggests that the growth of GDP will decline from around 2.8 per cent in 1988 to less than 2 per cent in 1990–91, that inflation will remain in the region of 5 per cent whilst unemployment remains stubbornly close to 3 million. The balance of payments will move into deficit and the pound will continue its protracted decline with its trade-weighted value falling to below 60 per cent of its 1975 value by 1991.

The comparative decline of the UK economy was probably well established for historical reasons. The Thatcher government has made a bold and consistent attempt to arrest and reverse that decline which it considered in part to be a direct consequence of misconceived Keynesian policies. In doing so, it has provided a unique testing ground for the application of monetarist and new classical policies in a manner which is without precedent in modern advanced economies. It is probably too soon to judge the ultimate consequences of this experiment. It would, however, be premature to suggest that it has signalled the end of Keynesian economics.

REAGANOMICS

In many respects, the economic philosophy of the Thatcher administration was remarkably similar, at least in spirit, with the views expressed by the incoming Reagan administration in the United States in 1980. Indeed, it was as if the trauma of the stagflation era had produced the same kind of ideological reaction on both sides of the Atlantic. The rhetoric of the Reagan administration was almost identical to views expressed by senior Conservative ministers and found expression in the call for the elimination of inflation, the desire for less government agencies, balanced budgets and, above all, in the belief in the virtues of markets, deregulation and supply-side strategies. If the philosophy and indeed the intention were remarkably similar, the practice and the outcome were decidedly different. In the event, the United States succeeded in getting inflation under control without incurring the degree of output and employment losses associated with the Thatcher experiment. There were two distinct factors accounting for the comparatively superior performance of the United States economy. On the one hand, the underlying conditions were relatively more favourable and more conducive to the implementation of the proposed policy measures. Thus for example, the American labour market exhibits much greater flexibility. A much smaller percentage of the workforce is unionised (approximately 20 per cent compared to about 45 per cent in the United Kingdom) and there is also evidence of much greater locational mobility. The comparatively high growth rates achieved in the southern United States (where wage rates are generally lower) have been encouraged in part by the influx of skilled migrant labour from the North. The greater flexibility of the American labour market would accordingly suggest that policies of aggregate demand restraint might exert lower costs in terms of output lost and employment forgone.

Again, the public sector in terms of GNP is smaller in the United States and there are fewer vested interests involved in its continued existence. State enterprises contribute less in percentage terms to GNP and there is a lower social acceptance of free public provision of services such as health and housing. The philosophy of the welfare state is less ingrained, as reflected, for example, in the reliance on Workfare programmes, and benefits in kind as opposed to in cash. Consequently, there is less opposition to the rolling-back of government which is seen as a crucial element in the supply-side strategy.

The fundamental reason for the different outcomes in the United States and the United Kingdom, however, lies in the difference in fiscal stance. In the United Kingdom, the initial deflationary package combined a strict monetary policy with an equally strict fiscal stance. Although direct taxes were reduced there was a compensating increase in indirect taxes and indeed initially the total tax burden actually increased. In sharp contrast, in the United States the effective policy combined a tight monetary stance to defeat inflation with a relatively lax fiscal policy which saw the budget deficit soar to record levels. Despite the expressed belief in annually balanced budgets, which had characterised the official announcements of the incoming administration, in practice the policy was deficit financing on a grand scale. How is this apparent paradox to be explained?

The Laffer Curve

First and foremost, it would appear that the Reagan administration displayed a touching if naive attachment to the concept of the Laffer curve and sincerely believed that a programme of tax-cutting was possible without incurring fiscal deficits. The philosophy of the Laffer curve, it may be noted, comes in two distinct forms – the comparative static version which relates fiscal yields to tax rates at a given point in time, and the more dynamic version which is couched in terms of tax incentives generating expansionary movements in output and employment leading to a widening of the tax base over time. The former concept is the one which has found favour in elementary textbooks and which is depicted below. The rationale for its construction is intuitively appealing but the policy implications which are then derived are less plausible. Stated simply, fiscal revenue is depicted as a function of the rate of income tax. With a zero tax rate, the tax rate is clearly zero; equally with a tax rate of 100 per cent the yield will again be zero because no-one will have any incentive to engage in taxable work effort. Tying the two concepts together we trace out a curve as shown in Figure 8.2 with a unique tax rate $\bar{t}$ consistent with maximising the fiscal yield. Now, should the actual rate of tax be t_1, it follows that a substantial tax cut to t_2 is possible without reducing the fiscal yield.

It appears too good to be true, and indeed it is. There is absolutely no reason why the tax function should be quadratic as shown in the figure. Indeed, it is very difficult to derive a simple macroeconomic model incorporating a primitive constant rate income tax which satisfies the first order conditions for a revenue maximum. If a maximum does exist, it is much more plausibly illustrated by reference to Figure 8.3 implying a much reduced scope for tax-cutting programmes.

A much more sophisticated approach to the philosophy underlying the Laffer curve phenomenon, however, can be

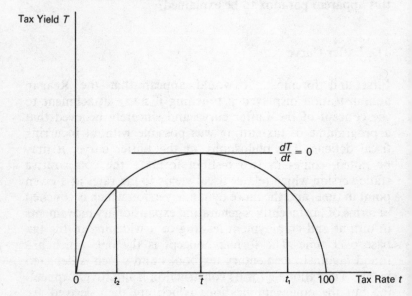

Figure 8.2 The Laffer curve in theory

derived from taking a dynamic perspective. If tax cuts provide appropriate incentives to greater work effort and risk-taking, and if they are accompanied by policies to raise overall efficiency by promoting competition, eliminating monopolistic restrictions and controls then they *may* be instrumental in promoting an autonomous raising of the natural rate of output and employment reflected in an outward shift of the aggregate supply curve. Such a raising of the natural level of output implies an expansion of the tax base. Thus, theoretically, it is perfectly possible for a programme of tax reductions to be accompanied by a progressive raising of tax revenues over time. Thus, although a policy of rate reduction might be expected to generate an initial rise in the fiscal deficit the longer-term implication may be consistent with the elimination of the deficit – a kind of J 'curve' effect in respect of the budget function. This more dynamic interpretation of the Laffer curve has more to commend it on *a priori* theoretical grounds although it may be noted that it contains nothing essentially new. Indeed, Keynesian-oriented economists have long pointed to the need

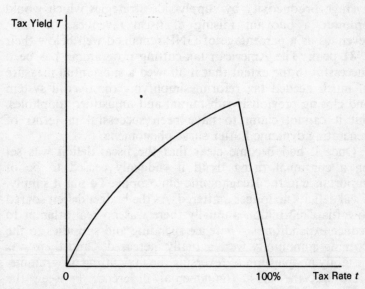

Figure 8.3 The alternative Laffer curve

for a programme of progressive tax cutting or increased expenditures to overcome the problems of 'fiscal drag' in a growing economy. In the event, however, whichever version of the Laffer curve one chooses to adopt, it does not appear to be applicable to the United States economy during the Reagan era. The tax-cutting programme enacted in 1981 led predictably to a substantial rise in the short-term fiscal deficit. Nor was this initial raising of the deficit to be countered by the long-term dynamic benefits of supply-side strategy.

The reason for the latter is not hard to find. Despite all the rhetoric there was no supply-side miracle achieved in the United States during the Reagan era (cf. Blanchard, 1987). Admittedly, it must be conceded that there was far less *to be achieved* from supply-side strategy in the United States than in the United Kingdom. Productivity per worker was already substantially higher. Trade union powers were less entrenched and less restrictive, and a far greater emphasis on competition and private enterprise already pervaded the American scene. Finally, the public sector was smaller and less amenable to a general shake-up to spur efficiency. Thus there was in the United States far less potential to raise average productivity by supply-side strategies which would promote a buoyant raising of fiscal revenues. In 1987, revenues as a percentage of GNP remained well below their 1981 peak. The American tax-cutting programme has been successful to the extent that it allowed a substantial measure of much needed tax reform, simplifying the overall system and closing previously substantial and unjustified loopholes, but it cannot claim to have been successful in terms of generating dynamic Laffer curve phenomena.

Once it had become clear that the fiscal deficit was set on a continual rising trend it suddenly ceased to be of importance in the Reaganomic philosophy. To put it simply, fiscal deficits no longer mattered. As the budget deficit soared towards £200 billion annually there was no real attempt to reduce expenditures – defence spending and subsidies to the farming community were actually increased – and there was certainly no question of reversing the tax-cutting programme. Here lies the most fundamental difference between the economics of the Reagan administration and those of the

Thatcher regime. The former never accepted the essential philosophy underlying the British government's view of the medium-term financial strategy. From the American point of view, it was perfectly possible for the administration to run record deficits without their being monetarised and jeopardising the fight against inflation. The link between the size of the fiscal deficit and the money supply was expressly denied. This, of course, was very much in keeping with Keynesian thinking – deficits could be financed by bond sales without inducing monetary expansion. For all the alleged consensus concerning the new conservative revolution in economic policy on both sides of the Atlantic, the reality was vastly different. In many respects the American economy was following fundamental principles of Keynesian deficit finance in sharp contrast to the hardcore monetarism being practised in Britain. And whilst this was not the only influence at work, it does in part account for the fact that American unemployment figures did not soar to the same heights, in percentage terms, as those experienced in Britain.

How was the budget deficit financed? In large measure, the answer justified the Keynesian optimism. Substantial external sales of American government bonds were made to Japanese investors attracted by the high rates of interest offered in relation to the low annual rate of Japanese inflation. High price/earnings ratios characteristic of the Tokyo stock exchange also attracted potential Japanese investors. For a considerable period of time, it appeared that the Reagan administration's confidence was fully justified. No doubt one cost of the large budget deficit was to maintain interest rates at levels which would not otherwise prevail, and this certainly had a knock-on effect on interest rates throughout the world economy. World economic growth might thereby be reduced but even this was by no means conclusive. Attempts to eliminate the deficit in the United States might allow lower rates of interest but it would most certainly provoke an American recession which would exert world-wide repercussions. The only possible sign of unease lay with the impact of the higher interest rates on the Third World debtor nations. The spectre of one or more developing economies defaulting on their repayments was not purely fantasy but a definite if distant possibility carrying horrendous implications of imminent financial collapse in American banking and financial circles. Even here, however, it was accepted that the problem of Third World debtor nations could not be solved merely by inducing a decline in the American rate of interest. More radical solutions would be required other than curbing the American budget deficit. Strictly speaking, therefore, Keynesians were justifiably confident of the success of Reagan's own peculiar brand of fiscal Keynesianism.

And so they might have remained had the American economy been entirely closed. However, the fact of the matter is that the American budget deficit was matched by an increasingly large trade deficit running close to approximately £10–$15 billion per month on current account! Sooner or later, a deficit of this magnitude must translate into expectations of a dollar devaluation which in turn must generate a substantial depreciation of the dollar. Which, of course, is precisely what happened during the crash of 1987, with the dollar going into almost free fall and the world's central banks helpless to prevent its slide despite costly buying sprees. Now the decline in the American dollar, of itself, might be no bad thing and indeed might be the required corrective to eliminate the trade deficit – although it would need the support of expansionary fiscal policies elsewhere especially in Europe. But one inevitable consequence of the dollar's decline was reduced willingness, even reluctance, upon the part of Japanese investors, to buy government bonds to cover the budget deficit. Suddenly the spectre of the fiscal deficit being monetarised, reinforcing the inflationary consequences of higher import prices as the dollar declined was sufficient to rekindle memories of the inflationary era of the 1970s sending world stock markets into turmoil. At last, the fiction of consensus in British and American economic policy was exposed once and for all with both Mrs Thatcher and the Chancellor of the Exchequer, Nigel Lawson, lecturing the American administration on economic policy – and in terms which would cause any Keynesian to squirm, namely on the need to raise taxes and reduce expenditures *in order to avoid a movement into recession*.

At the time of writing (end–1987) it is not immediately

clear how this issue will be resolved. Mr James Baker, America's leading economic advisor, has reaffirmed his Keynesian leanings by indicating a preference for a further decline of the American dollar in preference to radical expenditure reductions and tax hikes which might trigger recession. A raising of the world inflation rate might emerge in consequence but might indeed be the preferred alternative. One unlikely outcome would appear to be the issuance of American government bonds denominated in Japanese yen. Whilst this seems to be an eminently reasonable policy proposal it carries implications of prestige and status for the American President which he would intuitively resist. Whatever the outcome, it now seems abundantly clear that Reaganomics is as distinct from Thatcherism as chalk is from cheese.

9 Conclusion

The Keynesian revolution was a remarkable event unparalleled in the history of economic thought. It conquered the economics profession in less than a decade – as indeed Keynes predicted it would.[1] This is all the more amazing given the fact that today, more than fifty years after the appearance of *The General Theory*, economists are still divided and still debate the question of what was the essential message of Keynes. Nor was the reason for the immediate success of Keynes to be found in the policy proposals so implicit in his doctrine of a demand-determined economy for the same proposals, increased public sector expenditures, and deficit finance were already being propounded, particularly in the United States before the *General Theory* appeared. Why then was the conversion to Keynesianism so abrupt, so wide ranging and so complete?

There are two possible answers suggested by consideration of the philosophy of science. The first, in the tradition of

1 In a famous and oft-quoted letter to George Bernard Shaw, Keynes wrote:'I believe myself to be writing a book on economic theory which will largely revolutionise – not, I suppose at once but in the course of the next ten years – the way the world thinks about economic problems .... I can't expect you or anyone else, to believe this at the present stage. But, for myself I don't merely hope what I say, – in my own mind I'm quite sure.' (Moggridge, 1973, vol. XIII, p. 492) The degree of self-confidence, indeed even arrogance, in this remark is quite amazing especially when it is recalled that it required more than fifty years for the Newtonian revolution in natural science to gain universal recognition. But Keynes' confidence (or arrogance) was fully justified.

Thomas Kuhn, argues that the existing body of classical economic theory was in an acute state of crisis in that it could no longer account for the observed facts of massive and prolonged unemployment of the Great Depression. In short, the classical paradigm was in decline, and Keynes provided a new paradigm which was eagerly seized upon especially by the younger generation of economists increasingly disillusioned by the failure of the prevailing conventional wisdom. In this version, the success of the Keynesian revolution lies in the fact that it was truly in the nature of a scientific revolution and above all it was eminently timely.

This view has been refuted, particularly by Blaug (1986, 1987) who argues correctly that pre–Keynesian theory had numerous explanations to account for mass unemployment all pointing to market failure because of wage and price rigidities arising from cartels and monopoly power of trade unions, and on occasions mistaken policy on the part of the monetary authorities. In his view, the reason for the remarkably rapid conversion to Keynesian economics can be explained by reference to the criteria propounded by Imré Lakatos. In the Lakatosian view, a scientific research agenda swiftly gains adherents when it is 'theoretically and empirically progressive'. A research agenda is deemed to be theoretically progressive if it displays 'excess empirical content' when compared to competing theories. To display excess empirical content it is required that it predicts some new or previously unexplained fact.[2] If subsequent empirical investigation services to confirm or corroborate these new facts then that programme is also deemed to be empirically progressive.

In Blaug's view the principal novel prediction of Keynesian

---

2 The idea of predicting 'novel facts' raises certain difficulties. Such facts must not be known before the research programme is initiated. Theoretical analysis yielding statements describing already known facts does not provide evidence of their validity; rather it provides evidence relating to the competence of the person conducting the model analysis. What is required in order to be theoretically progressive is for the model analysis to point to facts not used in constructing the model itself, and ideally not not even suspected when the research programme began.

economics turns upon the concept of the multiplier and the fact that the value of the instantaneous multiplier is greater than unity. Although the multiplier concept itself predated Keynes (Kahn, 1931) this was none the less a novel prediction and an unsuspected implication of the particular consumption function which Keynes invoked. Moreover it provides the theoretical rationale for the notion already gaining currency that the government can in principle spend its way out of recession in a given time-period if it is sufficiently willing to incur the requisite budget deficit. Thus the conversion to Keynes, it is argued, is perfectly consistent with Lakatosian philosophy in that the Keynesian research programme was theoretically progressive.

There were doubtless other appealing features of the Keynesian message which assisted in its rapid dissemination and acceptance. In particular, the fact that Keynes moved away from strict assumptions of utility-maximising behaviour, which were in many cases untestable, and instead focused on behavioural statements which readily lend themselves to empirical investigation (and verification or refutation) was remarkably in keeping with the spirit of statistical research and empirical analysis that was a feature of the times. Indeed, although we have indicated that the insufficient attention given to utility-maximising behaviour, is a weakness in the Keynesian analysis, which later Keynesians have been compelled to remedy, there can be no doubt that the sheer operational nature of the Keynesian thesis provided an inestimable spur to econometric studies and statistical analysis. Finally, mention should be made of Hicks' seminal paper which translated Keynesian economics into the simultaneous IS/LM equation framework. This provided a general equilibrium approach to the problems of the macro-economy which was appealing in itself, but in addition it was couched in elementary mathematical terms which any serious student of economics could readily master and yet at the same time which conveyed a certain pseudo-scientific respectability to the entire exercise. All these influences combined to broaden the appeal of the Keynesian framework and in particular to convert the younger generation of economists.

The Keynesian revolution is now more than fifty years young. During that time its influence has fluctuated quite remarkably, quickly gaining an almost unchallenged ascendancy in the 1940s and 1950s, gradually being increasingly questioned in the 1960s and then degenerating as a research agenda under the assault of full-blown monetarism in the 1970s. And yet, it has shown an extra-ordinary resilience and ability to reassert itself and like the phoenix to fly again. Currently, Keynesian economics is enjoying a theoretical revival, especially in academic circles. How is this surprising longevity to be explained?

Herein lies yet another appealing feature of Keynesian economics. It has displayed a unique adaptability to the changing theoretical innovations and empirical findings that have developed over the last fifty years. A few examples will suffice. The introduction of the Phillips curve in 1957 was quickly assimilated into the Keynesian framework and in so doing provided an explanation for inflationary price movements which had hitherto been wanting. Secondly, the revolution in expectations theory culminating in the thesis of rational expectations, which initially appeared so damning to Keynesian orthodoxy, has now been accommodated quite happily into the Keynesian model analysis. Repeatedly, Keynesian policy proposals emerge from a rational expectations framework. And finally, the conflict with monetarism, at least in its moderate Friedmanite version, seems to have generated a greater mutual understanding and awareness of the opposing positions and even to have provided for a genuine synthesis between the two. Certainly, there is nothing in the current Keynesianism which is inherently in conflict with the concept of the long-term natural rate. The Keynesian revolution is far from complete.

References and Bibliography

Alberro, J. (1981) 'The Lucas Hypothesis on the Phillips Curve: Further International Evidence', *Journal of Monetary Economics*, Vol. 7, pp. 239–50.

Bailey, M.J. (1962) *National Income and the Price Level*, McGraw-Hill, New York.

Barro, R.J. (1977) 'Unanticipated Monetary Growth and Unemployment in the United States', *American Economic Review*, Vol. 67, pp. 101–15.

Barro, R.J. (1978) 'Unanticipated Money Output and the Price Level in the United States', *Journal of Political Economy*, Vol. 86, pp. 549–80.

Barro, R.J. and Rush M. (1980) 'Unanticipated Money and Economic Activity', in Fischer (ed.), *Rational Expectations and Economic Policy*, Chicago University Press, Chicago.

Baumol, W. (1952) 'The Transactions Demand for Cash: An Inventory Theoretic Approach', *Quarterly Journal of Economics*, Vol. 66, November.

Blanchard, Olivier Jean (1987) 'Reaganomics', *Economic Policy* No. 5, October, Cambridge University Press, Cambridge.

Blaug, M. (1976) 'Kuhn versus Lakatos *or* Paradigms Versus Research Programmes in the History of Economics', in S.J. Latsis (ed.), *Methods of Appraisal in Economics*, Cambridge University Press, Cambridge.

Blaug, M. (1987) 'Second Thoughts on the Keynesian Revolution', *Rassegna Economica*.

Bleaney, Michael (1985) *The Rise and Fall of Keynesian Economics*, Macmillan, London.

Blinder, A.S and Fischer S. (1981) 'Inventories, Rational Expectations and the Business Cycle', *Journal of Monetary Economics*, Vol. 8, pp. 277–304.

Blinder, A. and Solow R.M. (1973) 'Does Fiscal Policy Matter?', *Journal of Public Economics*, Vol. 2, pp. 319–35.

Brown, E.C. (1956) 'Fiscal Policy in the Thirties: A Reappraisal', *American Economic Review*, Vol. 46, No. 5, December, pp. 857–79.

Burton, John (1981) 'The Thatcher Experiment: A Requiem?', *Journal of Labor Research*, Research Monograph No. 1, George Mason University.

Burton, John (1987) 'Would Workfare Work?', The Employment Research Centre Occasional Papers on Employment Studies No. 9, University of Buckingham.

Cagan, P. (1956) 'The Monetary Dynamics of Hyperinflation', in M. Friedman, (ed.), *Studies in the Quantity Theory of Money*, Chicago University Press, Chicago.

Chamberlin, Edward (1933) *The Theory of Monopolistic Competition*, Harvard University Press, Cambridge, Mass.

Chick, V. (1983) *Macroeconomics after Keynes: A Reconsideration of the General Theory*, Philip Allen, London.

Clower, Robert W. (1965) 'The Keynesian Counter-Revolution: A Theoretical Appraisal', in *The Theory of Interest Rates*, Hahn and Brechling (eds). Reprinted with corrections in R.W. Clower (ed.) (1969), pp. 270–97.

Clower, Robert W. (ed.) (1969) *Monetary Theory*, Penguin Modern Economics Readings, Penguin Books, Harmondsworth, Middlesex.

Clower, R.W. and Leijonhufvud A. (1975) 'The Coordination of Economic Activities: A Keynesian Perspective', *American Economic Review*, Vol. 65, No. 2, May, pp. 182–8.

Coddington, Alan (1976) 'Keynesian Economics: The Search for First Principles', *Journal of Economic Literature*, Vol. XIV, No. 4, December, pp. 1258–73.

Cohen, I.B. (1980) *The Newtonian Revolution*, Cambridge University Press, Cambridge.

Council of Economic Advisors (1960) *Economic Report to the President*, Washington, DC.

Currie, David (1985) 'Macroeconomic Policy Design and Control Theory – A Failed Partnership?', *Economic Journal*, Vol. 95, No. 378, June, pp. 285–306.

Davis, R.J. (1971) *The New Economics and the Old Economists*, Iowa State University Press, Ames, Iowa.

Fender, John (1981) *Understanding Keynes: An Analysis of 'The General Theory'*, Wheatsheaf Books, Brighton.

Fletcher, G.A. (1987) *The Keynesian Revolution and Its Critics*, Macmillan, London.

Friedman, Milton (ed.) (1956) *Studies in the Quantity Theory of Money*, University of Chicago Press, Chicago.

Friedman, Milton (1968) 'The Role of Monetary Policy', *American Economic Review*, Vol. 58, March, pp. 1–17.

Friedman, Milton (1968b) 'Money: Quantity Theory', *The International Encyclopaedia of the Social Sciences*, Vol. 10, David Sills (ed.), Macmillan Free Press, New York, pp. 432–47.

Gordon, Robert J. (1981) 'Output Fluctuations and Gradual Price Adjustment', *Journal of Economic Literature*, Vol. XIX, No. 2, June, pp. 493–530.

Hands, D.W. (1985) 'Second Thoughts on Lakatos', *History of Political Economy*, Vol. 17, No. 1, Spring, pp. 1–16.

Hansen, Bent (1969) *Fiscal Policy in Seven Countries 1955–65*, OECD, Paris.

Hicks, J.R. (1969) 'Automatists, Hawtreyans and Keynesians', *Journal of Money Credit and Banking*, Vol. 1, pp. 307–17.

Hicks, J.R. (1974) *The Crisis in Keynesian Economics*, Basil Blackwell, Oxford.

HMSO, Committee on the Working of the Monetary System (1959) *Report*, Cmnd 827, London [The Radcliffe Report].

Hutchinson, T.W. (1968) *Economics and Economic Policy in Britain 1946–1966: Some Aspects of Their Inter-Relations*, George Allen and Unwin, London.

Hutchinson, T.W. (1978) *On Revolution and Progress in Economic Knowledge*, Cambridge University Press, Cambridge.

Hutton, Will (1986) *The Revolution that Never Was*, Longman, London.

Johnson, Harry G. (1961) 'The General Theory After Twenty-Five Years', *American Economic Review*, Vol. 51, May, pp. 1–17.

Kahn, R.F. (1931) 'The Relation of Home Investment and Unemployment', *Economic Journal*, Vol. XLI, June, pp. 173–98.

Kahn, R.F. (1972) *Selected Essays on Employment and Growth*, Cambridge University Press, Cambridge.

Kay, J. Mayer, C. and Thompson, D. (eds) (1986) *Privatisation and Regulation – the UK Experience*, Clarendon Press, Oxford.

Keynes, J.M. (1923) *Tract on Monetary Reform*, Macmillan, London.

Keynes, J.M. (1930) *The Treatise on Money*, 2 vols, Macmillan, London.

Keynes, J.M. (1936) *The General Theory of Employment, Interest and Money*, Macmillan, London.

Keynes, J.M. (1937) 'The General Theory of Employment', *Quarterly Journal of Economics*, Vol. 51, pp. 209–23.

Kuhn, Thomas S. (1970) *The Structure of Scientific Revolution*, 2nd edition, University of Chicago Press, Chicago.

Latsis, S. (1976) *Method and Appraisal in Economics*, Cambridge University Press, Cambridge

Leijonhufvud, Axel (1968) *On Keynesian Economics and the Economics of Keynes*, Oxford University Press, New York.

Lucas, R.E. Jr (1976) 'Econometric Policy Evaluation: A Critique', in K. Brunner and A.H. Meltzer (eds), *The Phillips Curve and Labour Markets* (Supplement to the *Journal of Monetary Economics*).

Matthews, R.C.O. (1968) 'Why has Britain had Full Employment since the War?', *Economic Journal*, Vol. LXXVIII, No. 31, September, pp. 555–69.

Matthews, R.C.O. (1970) 'Full Employment Since the War: Reply', *Economic Journal*, Vol. LXXX, No. 317, March, pp. 173–5.

Metzler, L. (1941) 'The Nature and Stability of Inventory Cycles', *Review of Economics and Statistics*, Vol. 23, August, pp. 113–29.

Middleton, R. (1985) *Towards the Managed Economy: Keynes, the Treasury and the Fiscal Policy of the 1930s*, Methuen, London.

Millward, Robert (1986) 'The Comparative Performance of Public and Private Ownership', in *Privatisation and Regulation: the U.K. Experience*, John Kay, Colin Mayer and David Thompson (eds), Clarendon Press, Oxford, pp. 119–44.

Mishkin, F.S. (1982) 'Does Anticipated Monetary Policy Matter? An Econometric Investigation', *Journal of Political Economy*, Vol. 90, pp. 22–51.

Mishkin, F.S. (1982b) 'Does Anticipated Aggregate Demand Policy Matter?', *American Economic Review*, Vol. 72, pp. 788–802.

Moggridge, D. (ed.) (1973) *The Collected Writings of John Maynard Keynes*, Vols XIII and XIV, Macmillan, London.

Musgrave, R.A. and Miller, M.H. (1948) 'Built in Flexibility', *American Economic Review*, Vol. 38, No. 1, March, pp. 122–8.

Muth, J.F. (1961) 'Rational Expectations and the Theory of Price Movements', *Econometrica*, Vol. 29, July, pp. 315–35.

Neary, J.P. and Stiglitz, J.E. (1983) 'Towards a Reconstruction of Keynesian Economics: Expectations and Constrained Equilibria', *Quarterly Journal of Economics*, Vol. 98, Supplement, pp. 199–228.

Patinkin, Don (1965) *Money Interest and Prices*, 2nd edition, Harper and Row, London.

Patinkin, Don (1969) 'The Chicago Tradition, the Quantity Theory and Friedman', *Journal of Money Credit and Banking*, Vol. 1, February, pp. 46–70.

Patinkin, Don (1981) *Essays on and in the Chicago Tradition*, Duke University Press, Durham, North Carolina.

Patinkin, Don (1982) *Anticipations of the General Theory?*, Basil Blackwell, Oxford.

Patinkin, Don and Leith, J.C. (eds) (1977) *Keynes, Cambridge and the General Theory: The Process of Criticism and Discussion Connected with the Development of the General Theory*, Macmillan, London.

Peacock, Alan and Wiseman, Jack (1961, 1967) *The Growth of Public Expenditures in the United Kingdom*, Oxford University Press, Oxford.

Phelps, Edmund (1968) 'Money-Wage Dynamics and Labour Market Equilibrium', *Journal of Political Economy*, Vol. 76, No. 4, Part 2, July/August, pp. 678–711.

Phillips, A.W. (1957) 'Stabilization Policy and the Time Form of Lagged Response', *Economic Journal*, Vol. 67, June, pp. 265–77.

Robinson, Joan, (1973) 'What has become of the Keynesian Revolution?', in J. Robinson (ed.), *After Keynes*, Basil Blackwell, Oxford, pp. 1–11.

Samuelson, Paul (1939) 'Interactions between the Multiplier Analysis and the Principle of Acceleration', *Review of Economic Statistics*, Vol. 21, May, pp. 75–8.

Shaw, G.K. (1983) 'Fiscal Policy Under the First Thatcher Administration 1979–1983', *Finanzarchiv*, Vol. 41, No. 2, pp. 312–42.

Shaw, G.K. (1988) 'Fiscal Policy under the Second Thatcher Administration 1983–1987', *Finanzarchiv*, forthcoming

Shaw, G.K. (1987) 'Macroeconomic Implications of Fiscal Deficits: An Expository Note', *Scottish Journal of Political Economy*, Vol. 34, No. 2, May, pp. 192–8.

Skidelsky, R. (1975) 'The Reception of the Keynesian Revolution', in *Essays on John Maynard Keynes*, Milo Keynes (ed.), Cambridge University Press, Cambridge, pp. 89–107.

Smyth, D.J. (1963) 'Can Automatic Stabilizers Be Destabilizing?', *Public Finance*, Vol. 18, No. 3–4, pp. 357–63

Solow, R.M. (1980) 'On Theories of Unemployment', *American Economic Review*, Vol. 70, No. 1, March, pp. 1–11.

Sraffa, Piero (ed.) (1951) *The Works and Correspondence of David Ricardo, Vol. I – On the Principles of Political Economy and Taxation*, Cambridge University Press Cambridge.

Stafford, G.B. (1970) 'Full Employment Since the War – Comment', *Economic Journal*, Vol. LXXX, No. 317, March, pp. 165–72.

Tinbergen, Jan (1952) *On the Theory of Economic Policy*, North Holland Publishing, Amsterdam.

Tobin, James (1958) 'Liquidity Preference as Behaviour Towards Risk', *Review of Economic Studies*, Vol. 25, February, pp. 65–86.

Viner, Jacob (1936) 'Mr. Keynes on the Causes of Unemployment', *Quarterly Journal of Economics*, Vol. 50, pp. 147–67.

Weisskopf, T., Bowles, S. and Gordon, D. (1984) 'Hearts and Minds: A Social Model of Aggregate Productivity Growth in the US, 1948–79', *Brookings Papers on Economic Activity*, Washington, DC.

Wood, J.C. (ed.) (1983) *John Maynard Keynes: Critical Assessments*, Vols. I–IV, Croom Helm, London.

Worswick, D. (1985), 'Jobs for All', *Economic Journal*, Vol. 95, No. 377, March, pp. 1–14.

Yellen, J.L. (1984) 'Efficiency Wage Models of Unemployment', *American Economic Review*, Vol. 74, May, pp. 200–5.

Index